my first
BOOK OF
MY BODY

my first
BOOK OF
MY BODY

Discover how your body works with
35 fun projects and experiments

SUSAN AKASS AND
FRANCES BUTCHER

CICO **Kidz**

Published in 2017 by CICO Kidz
An imprint of Ryland, Peters & Small Ltd
20–21 Jockey's Fields 341 E 116th St
London WC1R 4BW   New York, NY 10029

www.rylandpeters.com

10 9 8 7 6 5 4 3 2 1

Text © Susan Akass and Frances Butcher
Design, photography, and illustration
© CICO Books 2017

A CIP catalog record for this book is
available from the Library of Congress and
the British Library.

ISBN: 978-1-78249-531-4

Printed in China

Series consultant: Susan Akass
Editor: Clare Sayer
Designer: Alison Fenton
Artworks: Hannah George, except for
page 113 by Stephen Dew

Editor: Dawn Bates
Art director: Sally Powell
Production controller: Gordana Simakovic
Publishing manager: Penny Craig
Publisher: Cindy Richards

For photography credits, see page 128

Contents

Introduction 6

Chapter 1

YOUR SENSES 8

THE EYE 10

Investigating eyes 11

Pinhole camera 14

Other ways to test your eyes 16

THE EAR 18

Explore your ears 19

Helping you balance 21

Air pressure and ears 23

TASTE AND SMELL 24

Smell test 25

Taste test 27

SKIN 28

How good is your sense of touch? 29

Temperature test 31

Our hairy bodies 33

Chapter 2

YOUR SKELETON AND MUSCLES 36

THE SKELETON 38

Draw your own skeleton 40

Joint quiz 43

Broken bones 44

Flexible spine 48

HOW MUSCLES WORK 52

Growing bones and muscles 54

Meaty muscles 56

THE HAND 59

A robot hand 60

Chapter 3

THE MACHINE INSIDE YOU 64

YOUR ORGANS AND SYSTEMS 66

YOUR DIGESTIVE SYSTEM 68

Make a model of your teeth 69

Plaque attack! 72

How to make poop! 74

String model of the gut 78

BLOOD AND CIRCULATION 82

Make tasty fake blood 84

Make a one-way valve 88

Find out about your heart 90

Make a model of your lungs 94

Test your lungs 97

YOUR EXCRETORY SYSTEM 98

How your kidneys work 99

YOUR IMMUNE SYSTEM 101

Making snot! 102

Model bacteria and viruses 104

Chapter 4

YOUR CONTROL CENTER 106

YOUR BRAIN 108

Make a brain hat 110

How fast are your reaction times? 114

YOUR NERVOUS SYSTEM 116

Make a pipe cleaner neuron 117

Billions of connections 119

Memory game 122

A dream diary 124

Confusing your brain 126

Index 127

Credits 128

Introduction

Are you ready to have some fun and find out how your body works? Making fake blood from a fruit salad, modeling your digestive system from eating to pooping, and constructing a hat to help you understand how your brain works are just some of the many fabulous things in store for you. What are you waiting for?!

In Chapter 1 find out how your senses work; how your eyes, ears, nose, mouth, and skin take in information so that you can find out about the world around you. Activities include how to make a pinhole camera to understand how your eye works, finding out why your ears pop on airplane flights, and testing your sense of smell.

In Chapter 2 you will learn about your skeleton and muscles and how they work together to hold you up and let you move. Activities include feeling and drawing your own skeleton and making a robot hand that moves.

Chapter 3 is a long chapter because it's all about the working of your body—how your digestive system processes food, how your heart and lungs work together to take oxygen to every cell in your body, how you get rid of waste, and how your body works hard to fight disease. Activities include how to make a stethoscope and listen to your heart, and how to make a model of your gut.

Finally, in **Chapter 4,** you will discover things about the most amazing part of the human body, the part that is letting you read and understand this book: your brain. Test your reaction times, puzzle over optical illusions, and start a dream diary.

This book is full of diagrams to help you understand your body, as well as fascinating facts and lots of health tips to help you keep fit, stay healthy, and be happy!

You can't learn everything about your body in this practical way, but we hope you will get interested and go on to find out more. Two topics we don't cover are puberty (growing up) and reproduction (having babies). You need a whole book to cover these subjects properly and we didn't have room for them!

Remember that not everyone's body is the same. We all look different and have different abilities. Some of the activities in the book will be difficult for some children. For instance, if you are in a wheelchair, you won't be able to try the balancing activity or if you have a hearing impairment you might not be able to play the listening game, but there are plenty of other things you can do. You may also be much better at some activities than other children—some children in wheelchairs will notice they have super-strong arm muscles when they look at them in the mirror.

There is just so much to learn and find out and we hope you will soon discover just how amazing the human body is!

Project levels

Level 1
Activities are very
quick and easy to do

Level 2
May take a little more
time and concentration

Level 3
These will take longer
or you might need
some adult help

chapter 1
Your Senses

As a newborn baby, you knew nothing about the world. As you grew, information streamed in from your senses—sight, hearing, smell, taste, and touch—and your brain connected it all up. The activities in this chapter help you find out how your sense organs—your eyes, ears, nose, mouth, and skin—all work.

THE EYE 10
Investigating eyes 11
Pinhole camera 14
Other ways to test your eyes 16

THE EAR 18
Explore your ears 19
Helping you balance 21
Air pressure and ears 23

TASTE AND SMELL 24
Smell test 25
Taste test 27

SKIN 28
How good is your sense of touch? 29
Temperature test 31
Our hairy bodies 33

THE EYE

What color are your eyes? Do you have long eyelashes? Are your eyebrows fair or dark? You will have looked at your eyes thousands of times in a mirror, but how much do you really know about them? Do you know that each of your eyes is about the same size and shape as a ping-pong ball, but you can't see most of it? The diagram below is what you would see if an eye was cut in half to show all the parts.

Try the activities on the next few pages to understand more about what each part of your eye does.

Look inside your eye

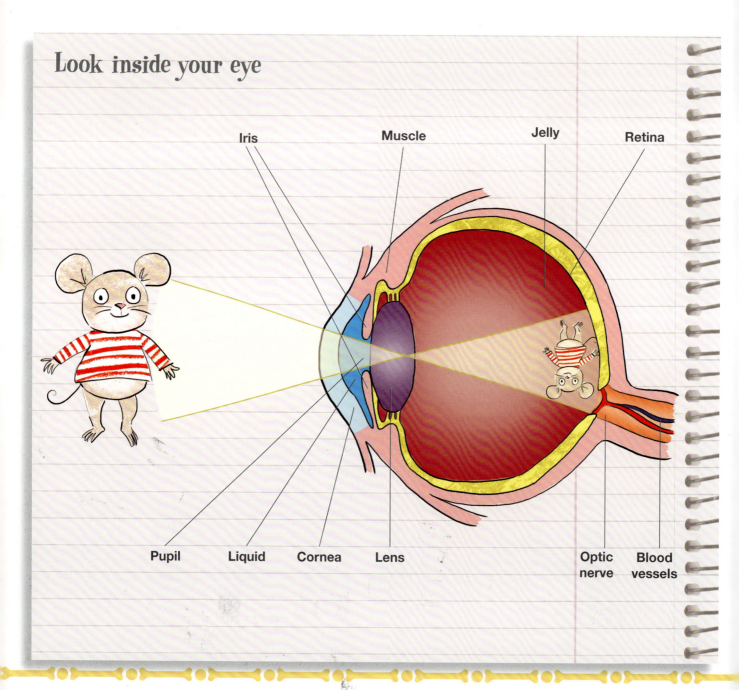

Iris   Muscle   Jelly   Retina

Pupil   Liquid   Cornea   Lens   Optic nerve   Blood vessels

Investigating eyes

Your eyes tell you most of what you know about the world. Just by looking, you can judge the size of an object, its texture, how quickly it's moving, how close it is, whether it's something or someone you recognize, and how dangerous it is. Your eyes communicate expressions, too, so start by making some silly faces in the mirror or try to outstare friends or family—who will blink first?

You will need

....

a mirror—you will see things more clearly in a magnifying makeup mirror

1 Take a close look in the mirror. Above your eye is your eyebrow. Run your finger along it and feel the hard bony ridge that is the edge of your eye socket (the hole in your skull which fits around your eyes—see page 39, Skeleton). This ridge protects your eye. Lots of children get bumps or cuts there, but don't hurt their eyes, which shows that it does work. The eyebrow can stop dust and sweat getting in your eye, but its main job is to communicate expressions. Make lots of different faces in the mirror and see how your eyebrows move to show anger, puzzlement, and surprise.

Express YOURSELF with your eyes!

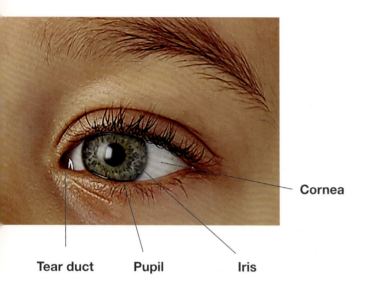

Cornea

Tear duct   **Pupil**   **Iris**

2 Now blink and watch your eyelids moving up and down. Your eyelashes trap dust before it reaches your eye. Your eyelids act a bit like windshield wipers when they wash a car windshield. Each time you blink, they wash the surface of your eyes with tears.

If you keep staring without blinking, your eyes become prickly because they dry out. Gently pull down the skin at the bottom of one eye and you will see a little dot on the inside just in the corner. This is the duct where your tears come from.

3 Look closely at your eye. There is a curved shiny, white surface with a colored ring inside it and a black dot at the center. Your eye is curved because it is the front part of your eyeball, which is about the size and shape of a ping-pong ball and filled with a kind of jelly. Most of your eyeball is inside your skull.

• The shiny part you can see is your cornea, which covers the front of your eyeball, like a wet sheet of smooth, transparent plastic, and protects it.

• The center black dot is your pupil, which is actually a hole that lets light into your eyeball. (Any hole in a closed box looks black—even windows look black if there is no light on in the room.)

• The colored ring is your iris, which controls the size of your pupil—if you are trying to see when it is dark, you need big pupils to let in as much light as possible; if the light is very bright, your pupils need to be small so not much light gets in. Too much light can damage your eyes.

• Keep looking in the mirror and move your head from side to side. Your eyes move too so you can keep looking at yourself—there are muscles moving your eyeball around.

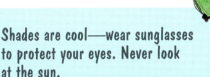

Health Tips

Shades are cool—wear sunglasses to protect your eyes. Never look at the sun.

"Stick and stones may break your bones"—but they are much more likely to hurt your eyes! They can cause blindness.

If you get something in your eye, keep blinking and it should wash out. Blowing your nose can sometimes help too. It's very tempting to rub your eyes, but don't as it can cause any grit to scratch the surface of your eye. If it won't come out, ask an adult to help you.

4 Watch how your pupils change—you will need a friend for this activity. In a bright place, get your friend to cover their eyes with their hands to keep out the light. Tell them to keep their eyes open and to look at their hands while you count slowly to ten. Stare into their face as you count. When you reach ten, they should uncover their eyes so they stare into yours. You should see the pupil shrink from quite big to tiny, but it happens very quickly so you may need to try a few times before you see it. Now swap places.

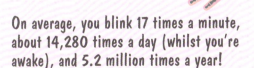

Fascinating Facts

On average, you blink 17 times a minute, about 14,280 times a day (whilst you're awake), and 5.2 million times a year!

All humans used to have brown eyes. People only starting having blue eyes around 6,000–10,000 years ago.

Pinhole camera

Discover how your pupils work by making a pinhole camera—it's easier than it sounds! You'll need to look out for one of the round snack tubes that have a metal base and a plastic lid.

You will need

long Pringles tube (or other tube with metal at one end and a plastic lid)

ruler

pencil

sharp scissors

thumbtack (drawing pin)

hammer

greaseproof paper

sticky parcel tape

aluminum foil

magnifying glass

1 First take the Pringles tube and measure 2 in. (5 cm) from the metal end in several places around the tube. Join up the marks to make a line. Use a sharp pair of scissors and cut around the line (or ask an adult to use a craft knife).

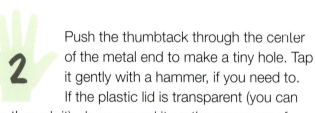

2 Push the thumbtack through the center of the metal end to make a tiny hole. Tap it gently with a hammer, if you need to. If the plastic lid is transparent (you can see through it), draw around it on the greaseproof paper and cut out the circle. Place the paper circle inside the lid and then put the lid on the short section you have just cut. Miss out this stage if the lid is translucent (cloudy) plastic.

3 Use the sticky tape to join the two parts of the tube together again with the lid between them. The lid makes a screen inside.

4 Wrap a piece of foil all around the tube and tape it together to keep all the light out of the tube.

5 Now hold the open end of the tube up to your eye and point the hole toward a bright window (never directly toward the sun) or lamp. Hold it tight against your face so no light gets inside. You should see a tiny image of the lamp or the scene from the window on the screen inside the tube—but it will be upside down! This is exactly what happens in your eye. The light from outside passes through the pupil and makes an upside down image (picture) on the retina at the back of your eye (see diagram on page 10).

6 Now put a magnifying glass in front of the hole. You may have to move it forward and back a little, but at some point you should a get a much brighter, clearer image of the upside-down lamp or window on the screen. This is called focusing. There is a lens inside your eye just like this. It doesn't move around, but muscles pull it so it gets wider or thinner and that has the same effect as moving it. The lens is there to make sure that the image is focussed on your retina. If it's not, everything you see will be blurry and you will need glasses— which are extra lenses—to help get the image to the correct place.

The image is upside down and you don't see the world upside down, so what happens? Your brain makes sure you see the right way up! The light rays hit special cells in your retina and these send tiny electrical signals along the optic nerve to your brain. The nerve is like the cable running to your television. The picture isn't in the cable; it's just a coded signal—it needs the electronics inside the television to turn the code into a picture. In the same way, your eye needs the supercomputer that is your brain to make you see.

Other ways to test your eyes

Why do people sometimes talk about their "blind spot?" And why do we have two eyes, not one? Find out on the following pages. Try these simple tests and watch the dot or the cross disappear like magic, and what seems like an easy thing to do, become quite difficult!

You will need

....

this book
2 pencils

The book test

Hold this book about 20 in. (50 cm) from your face. Close your right eye and look at the cross above with your left eye. You will be able to see the dot out of the corner of your eye. Now move the book slowly backward and forward a little way. At some point the dot will completely disappear! Try it with your left eye closed. This time look at the dot and the cross will disappear!

The reason it happens is that the special light-sensitive cells are everywhere on your retina, except where your optic nerve joins the retina. When light falls on this spot, you can't see it. It's called a blind spot. This proves that your optic nerve exists (see diagram on page 10).

The pencil test

This simple test proves that two eyes are better than one. Hold a pencil in each hand by your side. Bring the pencils up in front of your face and touch the two points together. It should be easy. Now do the same thing with one eye closed. Did you miss? It is much harder to judge how close things are with one eye.

Health Tips

Try to get your eyes tested about once a year. If you are having problems with your eyesight, such as having trouble seeing what is written on the whiteboard at school, make sure you ask your parents to get your eyes tested sooner.

Your eyes get better at judging the speed of cars and their distance from you as you get older, which means children are not good at judging when it is safe to cross a road. Always be careful on roads and use a crosswalk (pedestrian crossing) to cross the road whenever you can.

THE EAR

Everyone knows where their ears are, but the ear you can see is just the outer of three parts. It's known as the outer ear (pinna) and lets sound travel through your skull in a small tube (the auditory canal). At the end of the tube the sound hits your eardrum, making it vibrate.

You're now in the middle ear. The vibrating eardrum knocks against three tiny bones. The first looks like a hammer (malleus), which knocks against a bone shaped like an anvil (incus), which in turn knocks against a bone shaped like a stirrup (stapes).

Finally the stirrup knocks against the cochlea—you're now in the inner ear. The cochlea is shaped like a snail and is filled with liquid. The knocking causes a wave in the liquid and moves little hairs in it. The movement of the hairs sends signals down nerves to the brain to tell it you've heard something.

But as well as hearing, the inner ear helps you balance. The loopy parts in your inner ear, which are called semicircular canals, are filled with fluid to help you sense when you move your body—this helps you keep your balance.

Look inside your ear

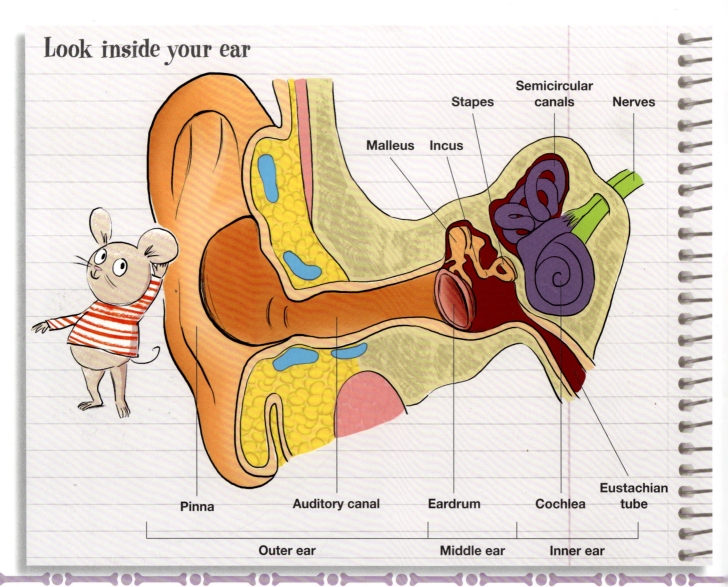

Stapes — Semicircular canals — Nerves — Malleus — Incus

Pinna — Auditory canal — Eardrum — Cochlea — Eustachian tube

Outer ear — Middle ear — Inner ear

Explore your ears

Try these simple tricks and tips to find out how different parts of your ears work. The marbles game is one that adults (teachers especially) will encourage you to play because it needs you to be very quiet. However, the noisier the better for the eardrum activity!

You will need

....

blindfold

2 marbles

small pot or jar with a lid

plastic wrap (clingfilm)

wide china bowl

fine salt or sugar crystals

metal baking tray

wooden spoon

Wiggle your ears

Can you wiggle your ears? Look in a mirror and try. Only some people can, but many animals have large ears that they move around freely—watch how much a cat's ears move. The movement helps cats direct sound inside their ears so they hear better and know where the sound is coming from. Try it yourself. Listen to a faint sound, such as a ticking clock or the buzzing of your computer. Now cup your hands behind your ears, facing the sound—it will be much louder.

Fascinating Fact

The bones in the ear were the first to grow to full size in your body. They were already adult size before you were even born, but they are still tiny—the smallest bones in your body—all three of them would fit onto one coin.

Can you hear it?

How good is your hearing? Play this game with a group of friends to find out. Sit in a circle and choose one person to sit in the center and be blindfolded. Put two marbles in the pot with the lid on. Pass the pot around the circle as carefully as possible, trying to make no sound. The person in the center listens for the slightest sound and then points at the direction of the sound. If correct, they swap places with the person who made the sound.

Good vibrations

Find out how your eardrum works. Stretch a piece of plastic wrap (clingfilm) as tightly as you can over the top of a wide china bowl, so there are no wrinkles. Put a pinch of salt or sugar on top. Now bang the baking tray with the spoon just above the bowl. Make a really loud noise and you will see the crystals begin to dance around. The banging makes sound waves in the air that spread out in all directions. They make the plastic wrap vibrate and that makes the crystals jump around. Your eardrum vibrates in the same way, but rather than making salt crystals jump around it makes the tiny bones inside your middle ear vibrate and hit the cochlea (see diagram on page 18).

Strange sounds

When you make a noise (speak, sing, shout) your larynx (voice box) vibrates in your throat. Feel it with your fingers. Sing high and low notes and see if you can feel a difference. Now try recording your voice on a phone or camera. It will sound very different to how you think you speak. That's because vibrations from your larynx travel through your skull to your ears, as well as through the air and that makes it sound different to you (see diagram on page 24).

Helping you balance

Scientists now think that we have many more than five senses and balance is one of them. It is your ears that let you balance so that you can stand upright and not fall over. The parts of your ear which help you balance are called the semicircular canals.

Feeling dizzy

Spin round and round until you get dizzy. Can you still stand up? If you fill a basin with water and swirl your hand in it you can understand what is happening in your ear. Fluid in the semicircular canals in your ear (see diagram on page 18) moves with your body as you turn, but when you stop, it keeps turning, just like the water in the basin keeps swirling around. This confuses your brain.

You will need
....

bowl of water

3 circular plastic bangles or hoops—they need to be the same size, but flexible enough to fit inside each other

Health Tips

If you have trouble hearing your teacher at school, be sure to get your ears tested.

Never poke things inside your ear— or into anyone else's ear! It's common for young children to get things stuck in their ears. You could also damage your eardrum.

Loud noises can damage your hearing— workers wear ear protectors in factories and building sites where noise levels are high, but many young people damage their ears with loud music, especially when they use headphones. Use noise-limiting headphones or keep the volume down. Don't stand too close to speakers when music is loud.

Balance test

Check how good your balance is. Can you walk along a narrow bar in the gym? How long can you stand on one leg? Don't just stand still, move your arms to test your balance. Then try standing on one leg with your eyes closed—you will soon find that you need your eyes to balance as well as your ears.

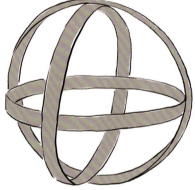

Fluid test

Take the three bangles or hoops. Hold one bangle vertically, facing forward and push another bangle inside so that it is horizontal. Now push in another vertical one at right angles to the first so it faces sideways. This is how the semicircular canals are arranged (although they are not inside each other).

When you do a forward roll it makes the fluid swirl in the first vertical one; do a cartwheel and the fluid will swirl in the second vertical one; spin round and round and the fluid will swirl in the horizontal one. Most of the time when we move, we don't spin right round so the fluid moves a little in different directions but doesn't spin and make us dizzy.

Air pressure and ears

If you have been on a plane, you will have felt your ears hurting or popping on take-off and landing. Low-pressure air in the airplane makes this happen. Try this experiment to see how.

1 Stand the bottle in the bowl. Boil a kettle and ask an adult to pour about 1 in. (2.5 cm) of boiling water into the bottle. Wait for about 15 seconds and then put the lid on the bottle.

You will need

....

sturdy plastic drinks bottle with lid (not one of the really weak ones)

large bowl

kettle

2 Add some cold water to the bowl and watch what happens. The bottle should cave in and crumple! This is because steam from the boiling water pushed out the air. When the steam turned back to water, there wasn't as much air in the bottle so the air pressure was lower. The higher air pressure outside the bottle pushed in the plastic.

The middle ear is like the bottle. There is a narrow tube that runs from your middle ear to the back of the throat called the eustachian tube (see diagram on page 18). It opens when you swallow, yawn, or chew.

When you fly on a plane, the tube will open and let the lower pressure air from the plane into your ear. When you land, the air pressure in the plane returns to normal and pushes on your eardrum like it did the plastic bottle. To stop it hurting, yawn or chew gum. Alternatively, close your mouth, hold your nose, and gently breathe in through your nose to equalize the pressure inside your ears and out. (When you take off, the higher pressure inside your ear pushes from the inside out.)

TASTE AND SMELL

We need to be able to smell and taste in order to know which foods are good to eat and which have gone bad and can make us ill. Most foods that smell bad are bad (although there are exceptions like smelly cheese!) Before you eat, you smell your food. That means you sniff the air around it and molecules of the food, which have floated off into the air, are sucked up your nose and over the smell-detecting cells. These are high up inside your nostrils in the nasal cavity (which is a space in the skull) and they send messages to your brain, which allows you to identify about 10,000 different smells.

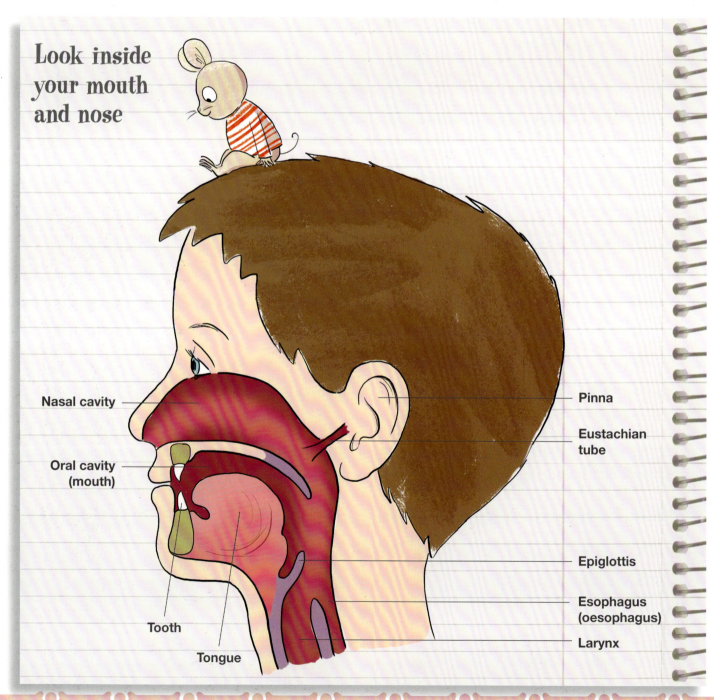

Look inside your mouth and nose

Nasal cavity

Oral cavity (mouth)

Tooth

Tongue

Pinna

Eustachian tube

Epiglottis

Esophagus (oesophagus)

Larynx

Smell test

Try this smell test to find out how good your sense of smell is—you'll need a friend to help you as you have to smell each item blindfolded!

1 Put a small sample of each of the different smelly materials into the cake cases. Label them so you don't forget what they contain. For liquids such as perfume, vinegar, and vanilla extract, put a few drops onto a small piece of cotton wool and put the cotton wool into a cake case. For mint, or other herbs, and pine needles crush the leaves a little before you put them in the pot to release the smell. Peel and crush a garlic clove. Cut off a small slice of onion.

2 To make the test into a proper scientific experiment, make a list of all the different smells in your notebook and draw columns beside the list, with one column for each member of your family or for each of your friends.

You will need

blindfold

about 10 foil cake cases or mini plastic pots

sticky labels

pen

notebook, pencil, and ruler

cotton wool

lots of different smelly items—here are some ideas:

—orange peel

—lemon peel

—pine needles

—coffee beans/powder

—tea leaves

—garlic

—onion

—vinegar

—mint leaves or other herbs

—rose petals

—pencil shavings

—perfume

—vanilla extract

—potato chips (crisps)

—sawdust

While you chew, you move food around your mouth with your tongue and you begin to taste it. Look at your tongue in a mirror and you will see that it is covered in tiny bumps. These are covered with taste buds, which send signals to your brains letting you taste five flavors: sweet, sour, salty, bitter, and savory. Every taste you recognize is a combination of these five, but flavor also depends on all those thousands of different smells you can identify, which is why food doesn't taste right when you have a blocked-up nose. You can see how your mouth and nose are connected in the diagram on page 24.

We have 5—6 million smell-detecting cells but dogs have about 220 million, which is why dogs follow their noses!

3 When everything is ready, blindfold someone, and let them smell each of the pots in turn. Tick the ones they can identify. Ask someone to blindfold you too so you can try, although it won't really be fair because you know what you put in the pots! Which smells were easiest to identify? Who had the best sense of smell?

Health Tips

We all love the taste of sweet foods like soda (fizzy drinks), candy (sweets), and cookies, but our sense of taste tricks us into eating too much of something that is bad for us. Too much sugar can lead to tooth decay and make you put on weight. If you're aged 7–10 you shouldn't have more than six teaspoons of sugar in your food a day, but there's about nine teaspoons of sugar in just one can of soda! Sugar can be hidden in lots of foods—take a look at the ingredients of your cereal, pasta sauce, or yogurt: How much sugar do they contain?

Don't pick your nose—this can lead to nose bleeds (and it looks disgusting!).

Use-by dates on fresh food help keep us safe from food that has gone bad but always sniff food and if something doesn't smell right, don't eat it.

Taste test

How well do you know your fruits? Find out how much taste is linked to smell with this simple test.

You will need
....

crisp apple

crisp pear

peeler

chopping board

knife

1 Peel the apple and the pear. Place them on a chopping board and chop them into pieces that are roughly the same size and shape. Separate the pear pieces and apple pieces on the board. Remember which is which.

2 Get some friends or members of your family to hold their noses, so they can't smell, and give them a cube of apple or pear to eat. Can they identify which it is? Get them to try it on you. Identifying taste isn't easy without smell!

SKIN

Your skin covers your whole body—it is the largest organ in your body and has lots of different functions.

Your skin has three layers. The top one is the epidermis, which makes you waterproof. It is made up of dead skin cells, which rub off all the time and get replaced with new ones. Underneath is the dermis, which is where your sweat glands are and hairs grow from and where there are millions of tiny nerve endings. The bottom layer is made of fat, blood vessels, and other tissue.

Look skin deep

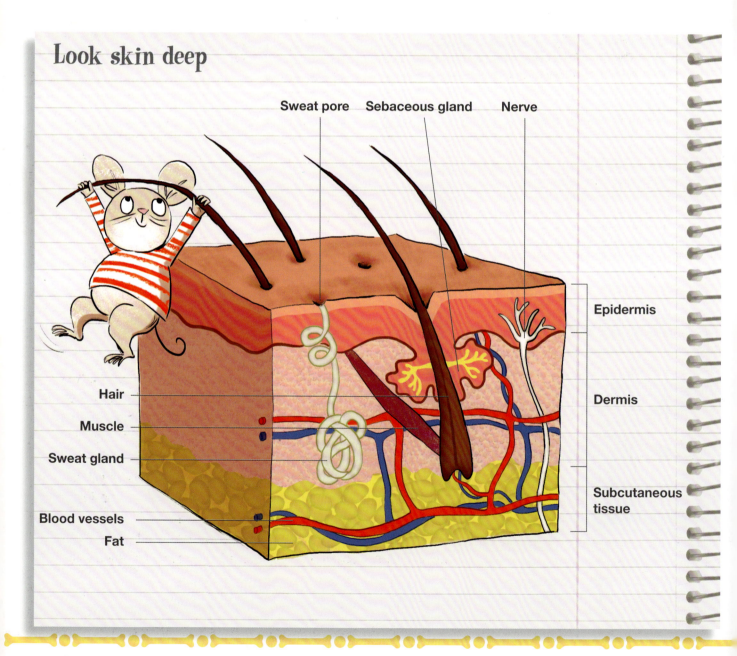

Sweat pore   Sebaceous gland   Nerve

Epidermis

Dermis

Subcutaneous tissue

Hair

Muscle

Sweat gland

Blood vessels

Fat

How good is your sense of touch?

A touch can be painful like a sting or soft like the feel of fur.
Nerves in your skin feel and send the information to your brain.

The nerve endings in your skin send messages to your brain whenever they sense touch, heat, cold, or pain. When you stand, nerves in your feet feel the ground, when you sit your body feels the chair, when you pick something up you know how firmly to hold it and, if it's hot, you know to drop it. Nerve endings fire with pain when you bang your funny bone or cut your knee. Our nerves keep us safe. However, in some areas of your body there are many more nerve endings than in others. Can you guess which have the most? Think about what you do when you want to find out about the texture, temperature, weight, or shape of an object. Now think what a baby does. That will give you some clues about which parts have the most nerve endings.

You will need

....

paper clip

blindfold

friend or family member

1 Unbend the paperclip and then bend it into a U shape with the two points about ½ in. (1 cm) apart.

2 Put a blindfold on your friend. Gently press the two ends of the paper clip on the skin of their arm. Be sure the two ends touch at the same time. Ask them if they can feel two points or one. (If you think they might cheat and say two when they only feel one, do it a few times and sometimes press with just one point.) Now try it somewhere else—try the palm of their hand, fingertip, top lip, cheek, and leg. Find out which areas on their body can feel two points easily. Now swap and let them try it on you. If you are being properly scientific, record your findings in your notebook.

Fascinating Facts

An adult's skin is about 2 square yards (1.7 square meters) in surface area.

Millions of bacteria live on the surface of your skin all the time.

The thinnest layer of skin is on your eyelids and the thickest layer is on the soles of your feet.

3 Experiment a bit further. Pull the ends of the paper clip apart a little and try again in one of the places where your friend could only feel one point. Keep widening the gap until they feel two points. Record what you have found out.

4 Scientists have found out that you can feel two points on your fingertips when the points are only a couple of millimeters apart. Your upper lip is almost as good but on your leg the points need to be more than 1½ in. (4 cm) apart before you can feel them both. Do you agree?

Temperature test

One way our skin protects is by letting us know when things are very hot and will burn us or very cold, which can damage skin. But just how good are we at judging how hot something is? Do this activity to find out.

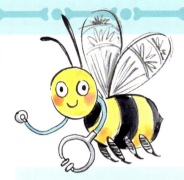

1 Fill one bowl with hot water from the faucet (tap). Add a little cold and then dip your finger into it quickly. If it feels too hot, you know your nerve endings are doing their job well and warning you that you will burn your skin if you put your hand in it. Add more cold water a little at a time until it is still hot but your hand feels comfortable in it.

You will need

....

3 big bowls
hot and cold water
some ice cubes

2 Fill another bowl with cold water and add some ice cubes. Dip your finger in this one. If it hurts it's too cold—again your nerves are doing their job well. Take out the ice cubes and add a bit of hot water so you can just bear to have your hand in it. Put the hot and cold bowls side by side on the kitchen surface.

Not too HOT, not too COLD!

3 Fill the third bowl with some lukewarm water—a mixture of hot and cold from the faucet (tap).

4 Put one hand in the hot bowl and the other hand in the cold bowl and leave them there while you count to 60.

5 Now put both hands together in the lukewarm water. How does it feel? For the hand that has been in cold water it should feel warm, for the hand that has been in hot water it should feel cold! Our skins are good at protecting us from burning or freezing ourselves, but are not much good at being thermometers and measuring temperature. You know this from swimming—on a hot day a pool can feel freezing, but if you are cold, the same temperature pool feels lovely and warm.

There are different types of nerves doing different jobs in your skin. The nerves that detect cold don't work when the temperature drops below 41°F (5°C) which is why your hands and feet go numb when they are very cold. The nerves that detect heat don't work above 113°F (45°C) because then the nerves that detect pain take over to tell you that your skin is too hot and will burn.

Our hairy bodies

One way in which we can identify an animal as a mammal as opposed to a bird or reptile is that mammals have hairy bodies. We are mammals so we have hairy bodies too. But in some places our skin is very hairy and in some there is no hair at all. Take some time to investigate hair. This is a good chance to use a microscope if you have one.

Hair detective

Use a magnifying glass to see if there are tiny hairs on parts of your skin you thought were hairless. There are no hairs on the palms of your hands, the soles of your feet, and your lips but there are hairs, some too tiny to see, everywhere else.

Goosebumps

Try getting cold quickly (for a few minutes only)—go outside without a sweater, turn the air conditioning on high (or perhaps put your arm in the freezer). Do you get goosebumps? Look at these with the magnifying glass and see that each one is topped with a tiny hair standing on end. Each one has been pulled upright by a tiny muscle that is attached to its base. The hairs trap air, which helps to keep you warm.

Animal hair does the same so animals look all fluffed up when it is cold. An animal's fur also keeps it dry because it is very oily and water runs off the oil. Your hair is also kept oiled by oil produced by sebaceous glands toward the base of every hair and as you get older you may find your hair and skin get oilier. These glands sometimes get blocked and can cause a spot or a blackhead—something else you might notice as you become a teenager.

Master of the microscope

Make some microscope slides of your own hair and that of your friends and family. To make a slide, cut a 3-in. (7-cm) long piece of sticky tape and put it down, sticky side up, on your table. Fold over about ½ in. (1 cm) of the tape at each end to make finger holds on the sides. Snip off a tiny piece of hair and use the tweezers to pick it up and put it on the sticky part in the center of the slide. Write your name on the folded side. Look at it under your microscope. Make more slides with hairs from different people. How different is their hair? Try looking at eyebrow hairs or hairs from your arm and compare them too.

Make a stink

Only do this activity with the help of an adult. Light a small candle or nightlight. Cut a few short pieces of hair (or pull some out of your hairbrush) and hold them in the candle flame with the tweezers. Smell the smoke. Now cut a piece of finger or toenail and use the tweezers to hold it in the candle flame. Do they smell the same to you? They should do because they are made of the same stuff, which is also the stuff which rhinoceros' horns and horses' hooves are made from—a protein called keratin.

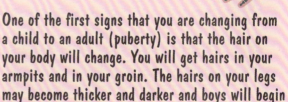

Fascinating Fact

One of the first signs that you are changing from a child to an adult (puberty) is that the hair on your body will change. You will get hairs in your armpits and in your groin. The hairs on your legs may become thicker and darker and boys will begin to grow moustaches.

Cooling down

We have seen how hair helps to keep us warm when we are cold, but our skin also helps to keep us cool when we get too hot. Let's see how.

Do some vigorous exercise—run up and down the stairs ten times, do 50 star jumps, or dance energetically to your favorite music for 10 minutes. Now look in the mirror. You will be breathing hard and you will be able to feel your heart beating fast (see page 91) but you should also see that your face is red. You will also be sweating and will feel hot.

When you exercise your body turns the food you have eaten and digested into energy. This is a chemical reaction that produces heat and the body needs to get rid of that heat. You are red because your brain has told the blood vessels in your skin to open wide and let more blood come close to the surface where it can be cooled by the air. You sweat because when water evaporates it takes away heat—think how much more quickly you get cold when you are wet after swimming. Sweat is produced by the sweat glands in our skin and it is mostly water.

Health Tips

The sun is your skin's friend and enemy. You need to let the sun shine on your skin because your skin makes Vitamin D, which your body needs to keep healthy. However, too much sun causes sunburn which is painful and damages your skin long term (you will be much more wrinkly when you get old if you have too much sun as a child). So get out and play in the fresh air as much as you can, but when it's hot in the middle of the day or if you are out by the sea or a pool, cover up, use sun cream, and wear a cool cap and shades.

It's important to stay clean. Have a bath or shower every couple of days to keep you smelling and looking good. When you hit puberty, you may find you need to shower more often.

chapter 2

Your Skeleton and Muscles

You know that there is a skeleton inside you, but do you know how many bones you have or how bones and muscles work together to let you move? The activities in this chapter will help you find out.

THE SKELETON 38

Draw your own skeleton 40

Joint quiz 43

Broken bones 44

Flexible spine 48

HOW MUSCLES WORK 52

Growing bones and muscles 54

Meaty muscles 56

THE HAND 59

A robot hand 60

THE SKELETON

More than 206 bones make up the skeleton that is inside you. You have more bones than adults because some of your bones, especially the ones that make up your skull, and your pelvis (hips), will join together to become one bone as you get older.

Without your skeleton you would be a soft, slippery bag of organs that couldn't stand up—a bit like a slug. Your skeleton gives you your shape and makes you strong, but it is also important because it protects the organs inside you. For instance, your skull protects your brain, your ribs protect your heart and lungs, and your spine protects your spinal cord. Your bones make you able to move. Muscles are attached to them by tendons. When a muscle contracts (shortens), it pulls on a bone and it moves. The other job your bones do is to make blood.

You probably didn't know about the last one. Most people think that bones are solid like a piece of wood or plastic, but they are living tissue and inside they are soft and spongy and contain blood vessels. In some bones, there is bone marrow, which makes new blood. If you have a dog, you may sometimes give it bones to gnaw. Next time, ask the butcher to cut one in half so you can see what's inside.

Look inside at your skeleton

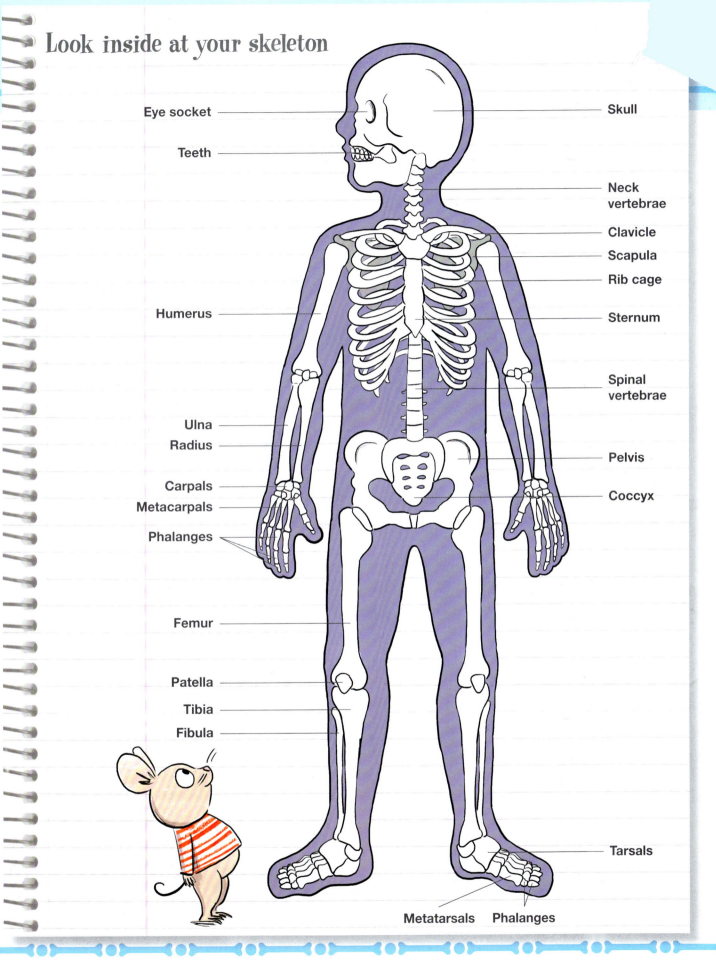

Eye socket

Teeth

Humerus

Ulna

Radius

Carpals

Metacarpals

Phalanges

Femur

Patella

Tibia

Fibula

Skull

Neck vertebrae

Clavicle

Scapula

Rib cage

Sternum

Spinal vertebrae

Pelvis

Coccyx

Tarsals

Metatarsals   Phalanges

Draw your own skeleton

How well do you know your own body? Here is an activity for you to get to know it a bit better. You will need a friend to help you with this one and, by the end, you will have a full-size picture of your skeleton. Remember that bones can't bend. Wherever parts of your body bend, there must be a joint between two bones.

You will need

....

roll of wallpaper
marker pens
full-length mirror
friend

1 Cut one length of wallpaper as tall as you are and one as tall as your friend. One of you should lie down on the plain side of your paper while the other draws all the way round you. Then swap so you have outlines of both your bodies.

2 Feel your skull. Are your nose, ears, and eyes made of hard bone? Feel the bony ridges around your eyes. How big are the hollow eye sockets your eyes fit in? Open your mouth. Feel where your jawbone attaches to your skull. Draw your skull inside the head of your outline. Your skull protects your brain.

Fascinating Fact

The longer astronauts live in space without gravity, the weaker their bones become. This could be a problem for space travel to Mars!

3 Feel the back of your neck and find your spine (back bone). Now run your fingers as far up and down your spine as you can. What does it feel like? Can you count how many bones make up your spine? Where does it end? Draw it in. Your spine holds you up.

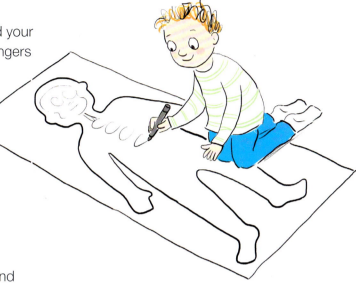

4 Feel either side of your spine and find your sticking-out shoulder blades. What shape do you think they are? Draw them in?

5 Feel around the front of your neck and your shoulders and look in the mirror. What bones can you see and feel? You need bones in your shoulders to join your arms on to. Draw them in.

6 Look in the mirror. Pull your shirt up and pull in your tummy as hard as you can. Can you see your ribs? Count them if you can. Your ribs protect your heart and lungs and help you breathe. Draw them.

draw your own skeleton **41**

Health Tip

Calcium and Vitamin D are really important for healthy, strong bones and teeth. Foods that contain lots of calcium include dairy (milk, cheese, yogurt), but also many green leafy vegetables, nuts, and seeds. Vitamin D can be absorbed from sunlight, which is why it is important to spend time outdoors.

7 Lie on your back and feel your hip bones. You need your hip bones to hold your insides up and to join your legs on to. Draw them in.

8 Now for your legs. How many bones can you feel in your leg above your knee? How many below it? Can you find your kneecaps. Draw in your leg bones.

9 Feet are very complicated. Take off your shoes and socks and have a feel. How many bones do you think are in your foot and how many are in each toe? (Hint: You might not be able to feel them all, but it's more than 20!) Draw your feet.

10 Now do your arms and hands in the same way, carefully checking the number of bones in your fingers and thumb.

11 Stand back and admire your drawing, then turn to the diagram on page 39 and see how well you have done. Why not cut out the outline and hang it up?

Joint quiz

A joint is where two bones meet. If our skeleton was all one piece we wouldn't be able to move and bend. There are lots of different types of joints in our bodies, but this quiz is just about two important ones.

Ball and socket joint
Imagine a big, round candy on a stick (lollipop) inside half a ping-pong ball that just fits around it. The stick can move in all directions as the candy (lollipop) turns in the ball.

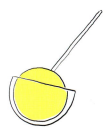

Hinge joint
Think about opening and closing the lid of a hinged box. That's all the lid can do—open and close. It can't move any other way.

Now try the quiz. Move your arms, legs, and fingers around and decide whether you have a ball and socket joint or a hinge joint in these five places.

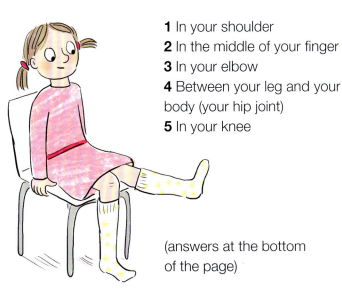

1 In your shoulder
2 In the middle of your finger
3 In your elbow
4 Between your leg and your body (your hip joint)
5 In your knee

(answers at the bottom of the page)

Fascinating Fact

When people say they are double-jointed it means they have extra-long ligaments. Ligaments hold your joints together. If your ligaments are longer and more stretchy, you can bend your joints further.

Broken bones

Lots of children break bones because children are so active and fall off things like skateboards, trees, bikes, and trampolines. There are different types of broken bone, some much more serious than others, but there are two types that children are more likely to get—greenstick fractures and torus fractures (fracture means break). A torus fracture isn't even a break; it's when the bone bends or twists. A greenstick fracture is when the bone bends and breaks on one side only.

But bones can't bend, can they? The answer is that children's bones are different from adult bones. A baby's bones are quite soft and bendy and they gradually harden as they grow up, so older children's bones are a bit bendy. When a bone breaks the body quickly begins to repair it—a process that usually takes around six weeks.

Try this quick activity to understand the different types of bone fractures and then learn how to put a sling on an injured arm.

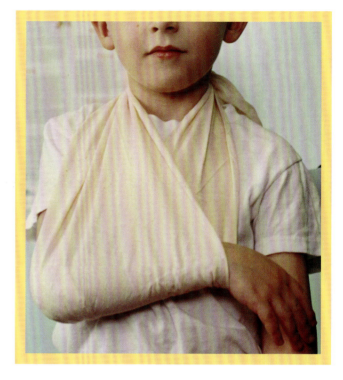

You will need

....

penknife

triangular bandage

 1 Go outside and find a bush or tree with thin, straight branches. Using the penknife, carefully cut one off (you may need to ask an adult to help)—if it is a living branch, it will be green under the bark and wet.

2 Next find an old stick that has fallen off the tree and dried out.

3 Bend the living stick so it folds but doesn't break. You will see the stick is weaker now. That's like a "torus fracture." Now fold it down harder until it begins to break on one side. That's like a "greenstick fracture" and you can see where the fracture got its name.

4 Now bend the old dry stick. It will break with a loud snap. That's what happens when adults break their bones and can sometimes happen to children too.

BONES can't bend, can they?!

How to make a sling

If someone has hurt themselves badly, and may have broken a bone do not try to move them. You can make the break much worse. Get help from an adult, who may need to call the emergency services. It is hard to tell whether someone has broken their arm, but if they are up and walking, and their arm is hurting a lot, it may help if they wear a sling. (If it hurts them to bend their elbow, don't try to use a sling.) This is how to put one on. Practice on friends and family so you know how to do it if ever you need to.

1 Get your patient to use their uninjured arm to hold their injured arm across their chest. Their hand on their bad arm should be higher than their elbow.

2 Open up the bandage. Hold it up so the long straight side hangs down. The point should stick out past their bad arm elbow.

3 Carefully slip the top point under their bad arm and gently pull the bandage up to their opposite shoulder.

4 Take the point that's hanging down and fold it up over their bad arm and up to their shoulder.

5 Tie the two ends together around their neck in a reef knot, with the knot at the side of their neck, on the bad side. (A reef knot is a knot that won't slip: right over left and under, left over right and under.)

6 Gently make the sling comfortable so that it supports their arm all the way from their elbow to the top of their little finger. Twist the tip of the sling by their elbow until it fits snugly around their elbow and tuck it in or use a safety pin to secure it.

Flexible spine

Your spine holds you up so it needs to be strong, but it also needs to be flexible so you can bend. Try making this easy model of a spine

As well as holding you up, your spine has another really important job. It's there to protect your spinal cord—a bundle of nerves that run from the brain. It is the main communication cable to the brain. All your other nerves branch off the spinal cord.

It's easy to make a model of a spine to show how it works. In the model the washing line is like the spinal cord and each egg cup is like one vertebra. See how it can only bend a little between each "vertebra," but each little bend adds to a complete bend. Your spine has 26 not 12 vertebrae, but some of the ones at the base of the spine are fused together to make one bone that does not bend. You even have a little tail of fused vertebra at the base of your spine called the coccyx.

1 Cut up the egg box so you have 12 separate cups.

You will need
....

large egg box

sharp scissors

wooden skewer (or a knitting needle)

piece of plastic-coated washing line

2 Carefully push the skewer right through each egg box cup so it goes in one side of the cup and out of the other, making two holes. Wiggle it around to make the holes bigger or use the point of your scissors.

3 Thread the washing line through each hole. When you have finished, line up the egg box cups so they are all bottom up.

4 Push the cups close together. Wind some sticky tape around the washing line where it goes into the first cup and where it comes out of the last one to stop the cups moving around and slipping on the washing line. Now bend your model around to see how it curves over and back and to the side.

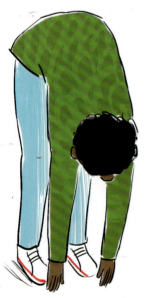

5 Now see how flexible your own spine is. Bend forward— can you touch your toes without bending your knees?

6 Bend backward as if you are limbo dancing or, starting from lying on the ground, see if you can arch up into a crab position.

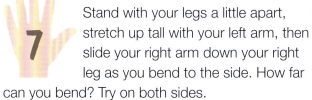

7 Stand with your legs a little apart, stretch up tall with your left arm, then slide your right arm down your right leg as you bend to the side. How far can you bend? Try on both sides.

8 Sit cross-legged. Put your right hand on your left knee and your left hand on the floor behind you— twist round as far as you can. Now do it on the other side. How far can you twist?

HOW MUSCLES WORK

There may be someone in your family who is often at the gym trying to build up their muscles and admiring them in the mirror. The muscles they work on are called skeletal muscles. (There are two other types of muscles, which we will come across later.)

Look at the muscles inside an arm

Skeletal muscles are attached to your bones with strong rope-like tendons. They can only pull, never push, so muscles at joints work in pairs—one pulls to bend a joint, the other pulls to straighten it out again. To pull on a bone, a muscle contracts, which means it becomes short and fat.

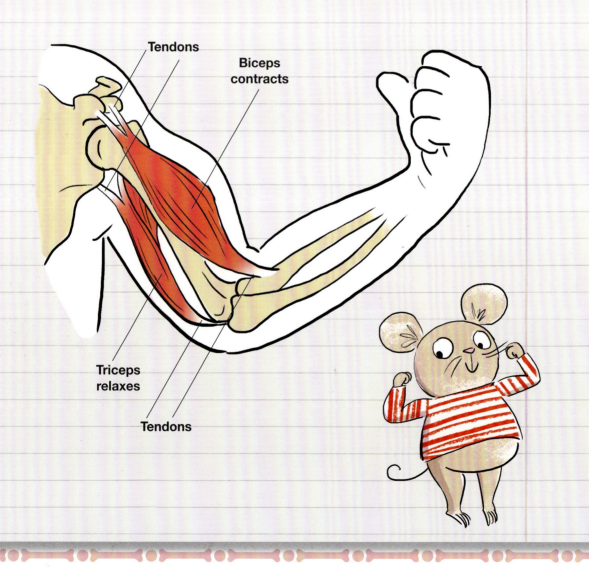

Tendons

Biceps contracts

Triceps relaxes

Tendons

Fascinating Facts

There are about 650 muscles in your body and muscles make up about half your body weight.

There are about 43 muscles in your face to let you smile, frown and make all those funny faces you practiced in Chapter 1 (see page 11).

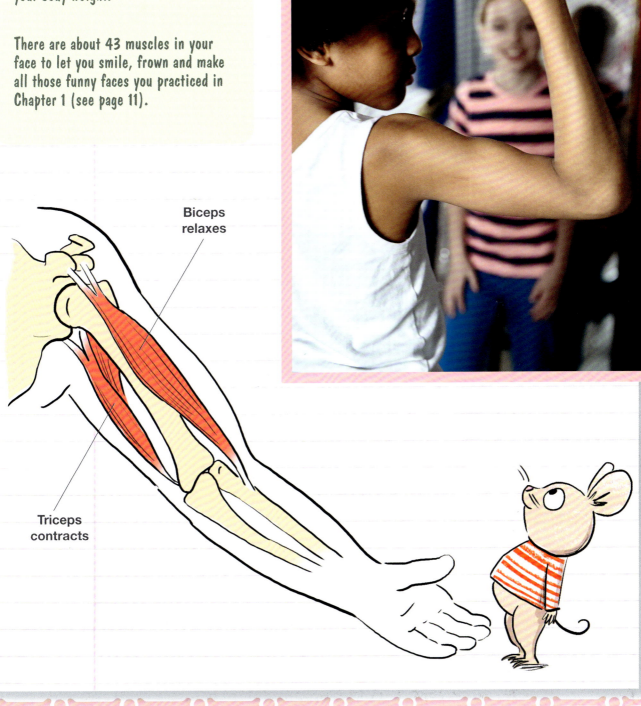

Biceps
relaxes

Triceps
contracts

Growing bones and muscles

Bones and muscles only grow and become strong if you exercise them. Your joints only stay flexible if you keep stretching and bending. Your bones, your muscles, and your brain can learn to work together at new skills, but only if you practice.

The most important thing to make you strong is to get outside to play running games or do sports whenever the weather allows (and if you can't get outside you can always put on some music and dance!). There are plenty of other things you can do to strengthen bones and muscles, stretch your joints, learn balance, and practice skills. Tick off as many of the activities on the list below as you can. Then target another one or two to work at until you can tick them off too—but don't stop after you have ticked them—keep improving so you can swim further, jump higher, throw better!

Try to do some new activities from each group—all of them will help to improve your fitness.

Improving my skills

- ☐ I can jump rope (skip) for 1 minute
- ☐ I can ride a bike
- ☐ I can swim 100 yds (100 m)
- ☐ I can ice skate/roller skate
- ☐ I can remember a dance routine
- ☐ I can keep a hula-hoop up for 1 minute
- ☐ I can catch a ball
- ☐ I can throw a ball more than 16 yds (15 m) at age 7 and 27 yds (25 m) at age 11
- ☐ I can climb a climbing wall
- ☐ I can jump a high jump bar set at 30 in. (75 cm) at age 7 and 39 in. (1 m) or more by age 11
- ☐ I can jump 1½ yds (1.4 m) from a standing start at age 7 and 2 yds (1.8 m) or more at age 11

Improving my strength

- ☐ I can get outside and play running games
- ☐ I can run 0.6 miles (1 km)
- ☐ I can swing along monkey bars
- ☐ I can do 20 sit-ups

Improving my flexibility and balance

- ☐ I can touch my toes
- ☐ I can do a handstand
- ☐ I can do a forward roll
- ☐ I can do a cartwheel
- ☐ I can do a crab
- ☐ I can leap frog my friend
- ☐ I can walk along a balance bar

Add more of your ACHIEVEMENTS. I can ...

Meaty muscles

One muscle bends your arm, one muscle straightens it again. Try making this moving model of your arm to see how a pair of muscles works together.

1 First stand in front of a mirror and bend one arm in a muscle man pose. With the other hand feel the bicep muscle on top of your arm bulge. To straighten your arm again the triceps muscle in the back of your arm has to pull your forearm down. Feel how the bicep stretches and flattens out when you do this.

2 Now cut two bone-shaped pieces from the cardboard—each about 6 in. (15 cm) long and 1 in. (2.5 cm) wide. Your forearm below your elbow is actually two bones—the radius and ulna—so draw a line down the center to show this.

3 Put the lower arm piece down on the table running right to left. Put the upper arm (humerus) piece on top to make an L shape, but about ½ in. (1.5 cm) in from the end of the lower arm piece. Hold the pieces together and push a brad (paper fastener) through both pieces of card where they overlap, to make a hinge—the elbow.

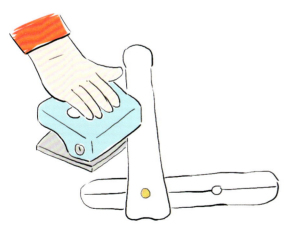

4 Use the hole punch to make one hole about halfway along the lower arm piece. Do the same on the upper arm piece. Thread a piece of string through the hole in the lower arm (with two bones) and knot it so it will not pull through. Thread the other end through the hole in the upper arm, but leave it free. This string is like the bicep muscle. Pull the free end and the arm will bend but you can't straighten it again.

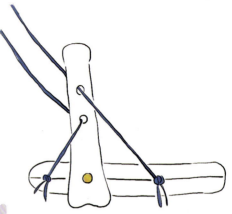

5 Make another hole right at the end of the lower arm piece where it sticks out, by the elbow. Make the last hole between the brad and the hole you have already made in the upper arm.

6 Cut another piece of string, thread it through the hole by the elbow and knot it, and then thread it through the hole in the upper arm and leave it free. This is like your triceps muscle. Hold the upper arm piece, pull this string, and the arm will straighten again!

7 Now sit on a chair and put your hand on your thigh. Straighten out your leg and feel your thigh muscle bulge. Which muscle bends your leg? Flex your foot and you can feel the muscle in your shin bulge. Which muscle do you use to point your toes?

Fascinating Fact

The jaw muscle is one of the most powerful muscles in the human body. It can produce huge amounts of pressure between your teeth when you bite. Dr G. Black of the Chicago Dental Hospital designed an instrument for measuring the power of the human bite called a gnathodynamometer—learn to say and spell that!

Who's the STRONGEST of them all?

THE HAND

How many bones do you think there are in your hand? Probably more than you think? Your hands are actually very complex structures that allow you to move your fingers and thumbs in lots of different ways so you can do lots of different things.

Look inside a hand

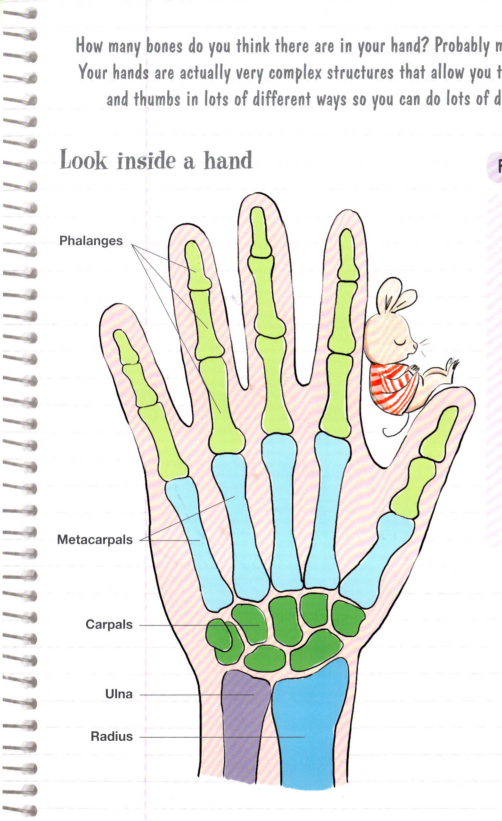

Phalanges

Metacarpals

Carpals

Ulna

Radius

A robot hand

This robot hand model will help you to see how bones and muscles work together—and you could even play tricks on your friends with it later! The model doesn't include the carpal bones in your wrist.

You will need

....

piece of cardboard (the back of a cereal packet would be fine)

pencil

sharp pointy scissors

straws (paper ones work best but plastic ones will do)

PVA glue

string

wooden skewer (or piece of wire)

sticky tape

1 Place your hand on the cardboard and draw around it carefully. Mark with a line where your finger and thumb joints are—two in your fingers and one in your thumb. Cut out the hand shape and then fold the cardboard where these lines are and then flatten it again. Put a dot for each of the four knuckle joints at the bottom of your fingers and another dot for the joint at the base of your thumb.

2 Measure and cut off pieces of straw that are the same lengths as your fingers and thumb from tip to knuckle joint. Snip a small triangle shape out of the end of each piece.

What can you make your HAND do?

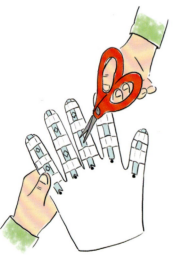

3 Glue the straw pieces onto the cardboard fingers and thumb with the snipped out triangle at the knuckle end and pointing up. Secure them more firmly with pieces of sticky tape but don't stick any tape over places where you have marked joints. These straws are like your finger bones or "phalanges."

4 Use the scissor points to snip out the top of the straw over all the joints. In your fingers there are separate bones meeting at joints. In the model we cheat and use one straw but make sure it can bend by snipping into it.

5 Cut five more pieces of straw to fit from the bottom knuckles to the wrist for each of the fingers and the thumb. Snip out a triangle shape at one end as before. Glue these pieces to the hand matching up the triangles at the knuckles. Leave the hand to dry. These straws are like your hand bones or "metacarpals."

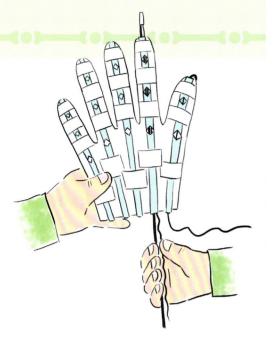

6 Cut five pieces of string each about 9 in. (23 cm) long. You need to thread these through the straws: to make this easier, tape one piece to the end of the skewer or wire and push this up through both the straws to the top of the thumb. Pull the string through (but take care not to pull it too far). Unstick the string from the skewer, and take the end of the string over the top to the other side of the thumb. Secure it with a piece of sticky tape. Do the same for each of the fingers. The string represents the tendons that are attached to your finger bones to make them move.

7 Gently pull on each of the strings to make the fingers bend. Can you make your model hand into a fist? In your real hand it is arm muscles that pull the tendons. Try making a fist with your real hand and watch your muscles bulge around your wrist. In your real hand there is a second set of tendons running up the back of your fingers and more muscles that pull on these tendons to straighten your fingers again.

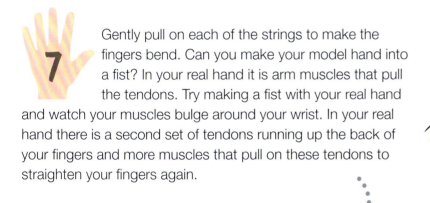

One thing the model can't demonstrate is your opposable thumb, which you can touch against any of your fingers on the same hand. An opposable thumb allows you to pick things up and do all kinds of delicate tasks. Try tying your shoe laces, writing your name, picking up a coin, or buttoning a button without using your thumb, to discover just how important it is.

chapter 3

The Machine Inside You

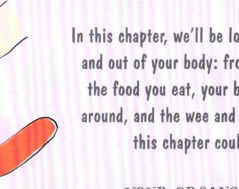

In this chapter, we'll be looking at what goes in, around, and out of your body: from the air you breathe in and the food you eat, your blood that carries everything around, and the wee and poop you make—be warned, this chapter could get a little messy!

YOUR ORGANS AND SYSTEMS 66

YOUR DIGESTIVE SYSTEM 68

Make a model of your teeth 69   Plaque attack! 72

How to make poop! 74   String model of the gut 78

BLOOD AND CIRCULATION 82

Make tasty fake blood 84   Make a one-way valve 88

Find out about your heart 90   Make a model of your lungs 94

Test your lungs 97

YOUR EXCRETORY SYSTEM 98

How your kidneys work 99

YOUR IMMUNE SYSTEM 101

Making snot! 102

Model bacteria and viruses 104

YOUR ORGANS AND SYSTEMS

Think of yourself as a bit like a car. A car has a body but, to make it go, it has an engine inside. To keep you going, there are different systems (made up of organs and other parts) inside you, which are like your engine. Each system has a special function.

• Your digestive system allows you to eat and digest food, and includes your mouth, teeth, stomach, and intestines.
• Your heart and lungs work together to get oxygen to your body, using your blood as a transport system.
• Your liver and kidneys deal with waste from your body.
• Your immune system keeps you well and healthy.
• Your male and female parts allow adults to reproduce (have babies).
• Your brain controls everything (we'll focus on that in Chapter 4).

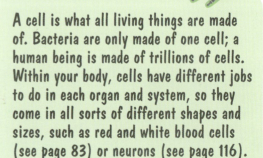

Fascinating Fact

A cell is what all living things are made of. Bacteria are only made of one cell; a human being is made of trillions of cells. Within your body, cells have different jobs to do in each organ and system, so they come in all sorts of different shapes and sizes, such as red and white blood cells (see page 83) or neurons (see page 116).

Look at your organs

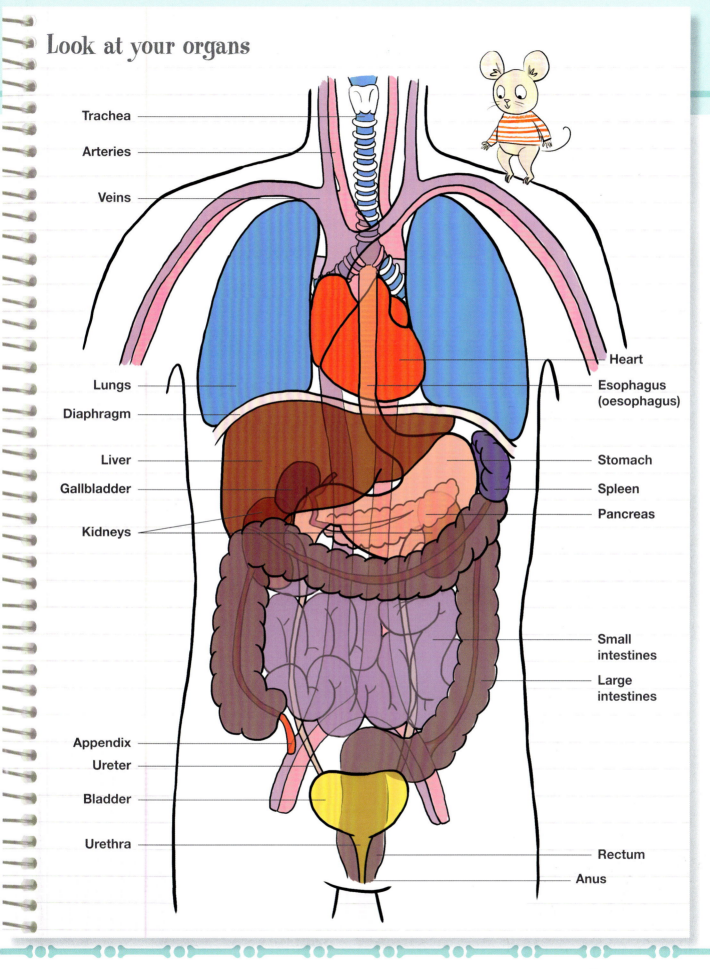

Trachea

Arteries

Veins

Lungs

Diaphragm

Liver

Gallbladder

Kidneys

Appendix

Ureter

Bladder

Urethra

Heart

Esophagus
(oesophagus)

Stomach

Spleen

Pancreas

Small
intestines

Large
intestines

Rectum

Anus

YOUR DIGESTIVE SYSTEM

Your digestive system starts with your mouth and teeth and ends with—poop!
It's all about what you put into your body and what comes out of it.

Look inside your tooth

The enamel that covers your teeth is very hard—this is so your teeth don't break when you bite and chew. Inside there is dentin—living tissue that contains tiny tubes leading through to the pulp, the soft inside where there are nerves and blood vessels. If your enamel is damaged, heat or cold will travel through these tubes to the nerve and your tooth will begin to hurt. Like your bones, your enamel is made mostly from a mineral called calcium.

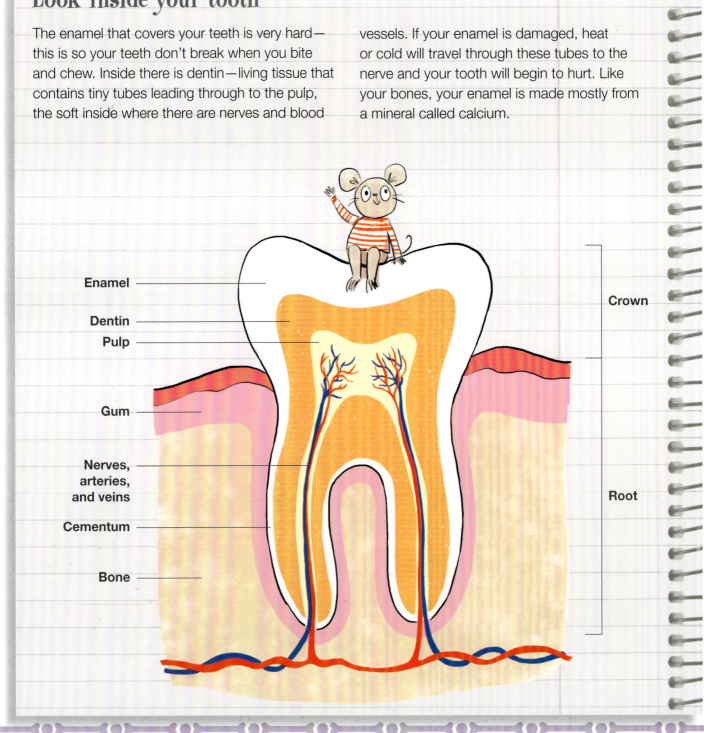

Enamel

Dentin

Pulp

Crown

Gum

Nerves, arteries, and veins

Cementum

Bone

Root

Make a model of your teeth

The first part of your digestive system is your mouth where your teeth do a very important job—cutting your food into pieces and grinding it up so digestion can begin.

The number of teeth you have in your mouth will depend on how old you are. You only have 20 milk (baby) teeth. When you are about six years old, the first of your adult teeth begin to grow under these and this will make one of your front teeth become wobbly and fall out (with a bit of wiggling help from you). Gradually your milk teeth are replaced with adult teeth and also extra teeth grow – some not until you are 18 years old or older. Adults have 32 teeth and these are called permanent teeth. If you look after them, they will last a lifetime.

You will need

....

modeling clay in red and white, or in different colors

mirror

tools to help you model, such as a blunt knife and a short wooden skewer

1 Roll out two fat sausages of red or pink modeling clay each about 6 in. (15 cm) long and bend them both into C shapes. These represent your upper and lower jaw with the gums over them.

2

Use the mirror to look inside your mouth. First look at your front teeth. These are incisors. They are quite square and thin like a blade. They are used to bite off pieces of your food. Bite a piece of apple to see how you use them. Unless some of your milk teeth have come out, you will have eight incisors—four at the top and four at the bottom. Use white clay (or choose a color) to make eight of these. Each one has a pointed root, which fixes it into your jaw.

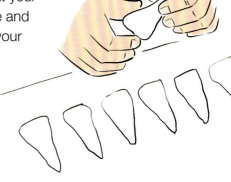

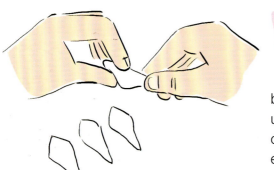

3

The next teeth are your canine teeth. These are your pointy vampire teeth, which are used for tearing off food. You have four of them—one at each side, at the top and bottom. Try biting off some crusty bread to see how you use them. Make four canine teeth in white or a different color from the incisors. These also have one root that is extra long because canine teeth need to be strong.

4

The next teeth, depending on your age, are pre-molars and molars. Molars are big, fat, cube-like teeth with four bumps in the corners. They grind together, crushing your food into small pieces—like when you grind up spices in a pestle and mortar. Children have eight molars. You only get pre-molars when you are about 10 years old. They grow next to your canines and are smaller than molars and also have a bumpy surface, as if they have been pushed down in the middle. (Adults have eight premolars and six molars.) Count how many molars and pre-molars you have and make that many. Molars have two big pointed roots to hold them in your jaw. Pre-molars only have one.

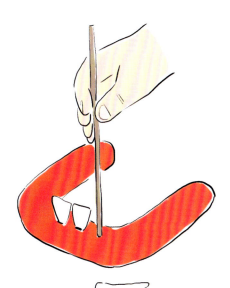

5 Fix each of your teeth into the correct positions in the curved jaw pieces, using the wooden skewer to make holes to drop the root into. Remember to leave gaps if you have teeth missing!

Keep those teeth **SPARKLING** clean!

Plaque attack!

Find out how plaque and acid affect your teeth by doing these simple experiments using an eggshell, vinegar, and some disclosing tablets.

You will need

....

egg

saucepan

white vinegar

small bowl

slotted spoon

paper towels

plaque disclosing tablets
(available from pharmacies
and dentists)

timer or watch

toothbrush

toothpaste

Health Tips

Have regular check-ups
at the dentist.

Brush your teeth twice a
day for 2 minutes with
a fluoride toothpaste.

Egg test

1 Put an egg into a pan of cold water and ask an adult to help you bring it to the boil. Boil it for about 12 minutes, so that it is solid inside. The eggshell is a bit like the hard enamel of your tooth, protecting the soft egg inside.

2 Carefully take the egg out of the water and put it into the bowl. Pour vinegar into the bowl until the egg is completely covered. We are using vinegar to represent the acid you get on your teeth when you don't clean them. The acid on your teeth comes from the slimy coating called plaque, which is full of bacteria. Every time you eat sugar, the bacteria turn some of it into an acid, like the vinegar.

3 Watch the egg in the vinegar. Can you see it is covered in tiny bubble? These bubbles are carbon dioxide, which is a gas produced when acid reacts with the eggshell. Leave the egg in the vinegar for 48 hours.

4 After 48 hours, lift the egg from the vinegar with the slotted spoon. Put it down on some paper towel and dry it. Now squeeze it and bounce it! The hard shell has become soft. Your teeth will never become soft like this because tooth enamel is much harder than eggshell, but, if you don't brush your teeth, acid from plaque will begin to eat away at the enamel, causing tiny cavities (holes). When there is a hole in the enamel, the softer dentin underneath is eaten away even more quickly to make a bigger cavity. The more often you eat or drink sugary things, the more chance there will be of getting cavities.

Check your plaque

Before you next brush your teeth, check how much plaque you have on them by chewing one of the disclosing tablets. (Follow the instructions on the packet and then look in the mirror.) The tablet contains a dye that stains the plaque bright purple or red. Now brush your teeth and time how long it takes to brush the stained areas clean. However long it takes is the length of time you should brush your teeth for twice a day!

How to make poop!

This is a messy activity guaranteed to disgust you, but it's brilliant fun. It's all about how digestion works and, as everyone knows, digestion ends up with poop.

You will need

shallow bowl or oven dish

3–4 slices of stale bread

scissors

cooked peas, beans, or sweetcorn

water

potato masher

large ziplock food bag

vinegar

red and green food coloring

leg cut from an old pair of pantyhose (tights) with the toe cut off

large old sock with the toe cut off (optional)

large plastic bowl

tray

paper towels

friend

Let's begin with the science: you need food for two reasons. First, to give you energy (like a car needs fuel) and second to give you the materials you need to grow, make repairs, and renew bits of yourself throughout your life. The problem here is that the food you eat cannot get to the parts of your body that need it without first being digested. During digestion, food is broken down into nutrients, which can pass into your blood and be transported to every cell of your body.

In this activity (you'll need a friend to help you), you model what happens inside your guts using simple ingredients and equipment from your kitchen. Each step is one of the stages of digestion.

1 When you eat, the first thing you do is to bite off pieces of food—use the scissors instead of your teeth and cut off pieces of bread so that they drop into the shallow bowl. Add a few spoonfuls of peas (or beans or corn) to complete your meal. The bowl represents your mouth.

Health Tips

Many people think of bacteria as the bad guys who make us ill, but not all bacteria are bad. In fact, bacteria are really important for keeping you healthy. About 500–1,000 different species of bacteria live in your large intestine, munching on any food that gets all the way down there and releasing important chemicals which your body needs, like calcium to make your bones strong and vitamins, which you need to be healthy.

Eat lots of different fruit, vegetables, fruit, yogurt, and cheese to make sure you have lots of healthy bacteria inside of you.

Don't be embarrassed to talk about pooping! There is no set number of times you should poop in a week, but if you don't poop very often and it becomes uncomfortable, then it probably means you are constipated. For muscles to squeeze food through a long gut, they need to have something to squeeze against. That's why you need fiber in your diet. Fiber doesn't get digested, but it helps carry everything along and out at the other end.

Fiber is found in food such as fruit and vegetables, baked beans, lentils, whole-wheat cereals, and bread. Eat plenty of these foods and drink plenty of water and pooping should not be a problem, but talk to an adult if it still is.

2 In your mouth, saliva (spit) is mixed with the food so add about half a cup of water to the bowl.

3 Your back teeth (molars) then grind the food into small pieces—use a potato masher for this, mashing everything together until it is a sloppy mess. Add a bit more water if you need to.

4 Next you swallow and the food passes down your esophagus (oesophagus) into your stomach. The ziplock bag is a model of your stomach so tip everything into the bag. Ask your friend to hold the bag as you do this.

5 In your stomach, acid and enzymes (chemicals) are added that break down the food into nutrients, which can be absorbed into your body. You can add a good shake of vinegar (which is a weak acid) and a few drops each of red and green food coloring. This should make it brown. Zip up the bag to seal it.

6 Your stomach squeezes and mixes the food into a soupy liquid called "chyme." You can use your hands to squeeze and mush the food in the bag until it is all liquid— the peas (or beans or corn) will stay whole.

7 When the food is small enough (after several hours), it is squeezed down into the small intestine, which is a very long tube, coiled up inside you. The leg from the pantyhose (tights) is a model for this. Working together, cut off the bottom corner of the "stomach" bag and squeeze the "chyme" into the pantyhose (tights). Do this over a large bowl.

8 Inside the small intestine, more chemicals are added to the chyme from your pancreas and liver, but you're not doing that. The chyme is pushed along the small intestine by waves of muscle. This is the second type of muscle that you have in your body and is called smooth muscle. Unlike your skeletal muscles (see page 52), they are controlled automatically by your brain. These muscles begin to work as soon as you swallow so you never have to think about food squeezing through your gut. Show the muscles working by squeezing the top of the pantyhose (tights) and pushing the food along with your hands. As it moves, all the food that has been broken down into nutrients passes through the wall of the intestine into the blood stream. You will see some of the liquid drip through the pantyhose (tights) into the bowl as it moves along.

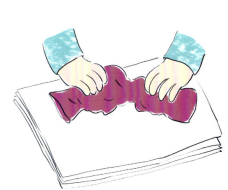

9 The remaining food moves on into the large intestine. This is shorter but wider than the small intestine. In here, bacteria break it down some more and our bodies suck out most of the water. Use a sock with the toe cut off for this and squeeze the "chyme" from the pantyhose (tights) into the sock. (You could miss out this stage if things are getting messy and just stick with the pantyhose/tights leg.) You can't really model the bacteria working, but we can take out some water. To do this lay some layers of paper towel on the tray, lay the sock (tight leg) on top and roll it up tightly, squeezing as you go. Some of the water will be absorbed by the paper towel.

Fascinating Fact

You are full of alien life! It's hard to know how to count them, but scientists estimate that you have roughly the same number of bacteria in your body as you have cells in your body. For an average person, that's more than 30 trillion (30,000,000,000,000) bacteria!

10 And what have you got left? All the things that the body doesn't want or need mixed with some water. Poop! Squeeze it out of the toe of the sock (anus) into the "toilet" (waste bin).

String model of the gut

In the previous activity the pantyhose leg and sock together are not very long. To get an idea of how long the gut inside you really is, you need to make a string model. This is easy and much less messy than the digestion project and it will amaze you!

You will need

2–3 types of string

scissors

small plastic bag

plastic carrier bag

thicker rope or string

sheet of wallpaper or other paper as tall as you are

friend

marker pen

sticky tack or tape

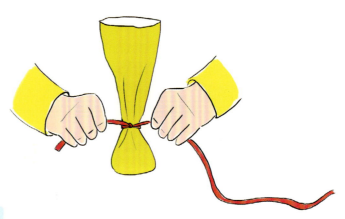

1 Cut a 14-in. (35-cm) piece of string for the esophagus/oesophagus (your throat and the tube to your stomach). Tie one end round the bottom of the small plastic bag so that the plastic bag (your mouth) is only 3 in. (8 cm) long. Trim off the extra bag length.

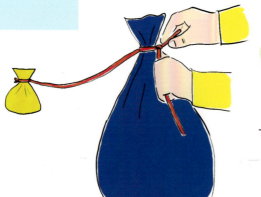

2 Tie the other end of the "esophagus" to the top of the carrier bag. Tie the string so it ends up 10 in. (25 cm) long. The carrier bag represents your stomach.

You'll be AMAZED how long your gut is!

Your trachea (windpipe) and your esophagus (oesophagus) both lead from your throat; the windpipe goes to your lungs, the esophagus to your stomach. To stop food going down the wrong tube and into your lung, there is a flap called the epiglottis (see page 24), which blocks your windpipe when you swallow. Sometimes this doesn't work properly and you choke and have to cough up the food that went the wrong way.

If someone's windpipe is completely blocked, they won't be able to breathe at all. This is an emergency and you need to get help very quickly. Sometimes hitting them firmly between the shoulder blades can move the piece of food, but call for help before you try this.

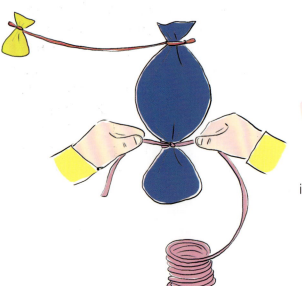

3 Cut another piece of string that is 15 feet (4.5 m) long. This really, really long piece is your small intestine. Tie one end around the end of stomach bag so the stomach is 6 in. (15 cm) long. Trim off the extra bag length.

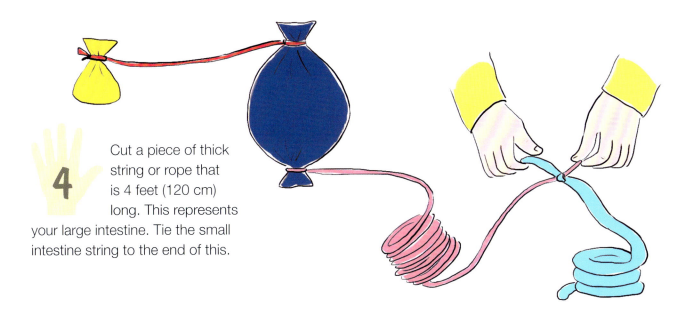

4 Cut a piece of thick string or rope that is 4 feet (120 cm) long. This represents your large intestine. Tie the small intestine string to the end of this.

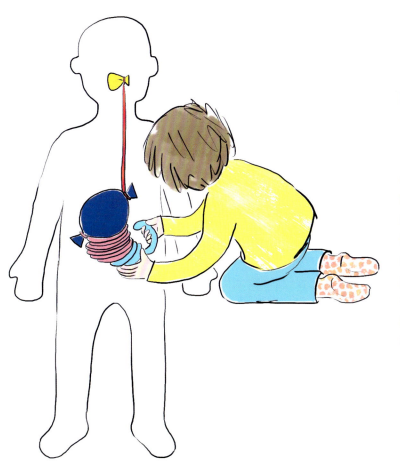

5 Stretch it all out and see just how long it is. Now lie down on the paper and get someone else to draw around you. (If you have made the skeleton drawing on page 40, you already have a body to fit your guts inside!) Use the diagram of your organs on page 67 as a guide to arrange the guts inside your body. Use pieces of sticky tack or tape to hold bits in place. The mouth bag will have to go sideways. Can you get it all to fit?

BLOOD AND CIRCULATION

Your heart, lungs, and blood make up a non-stop transport system in which your heart keeps pumping blood, and the blood takes oxygen from the lungs to every cell in your body.

Look inside your heart

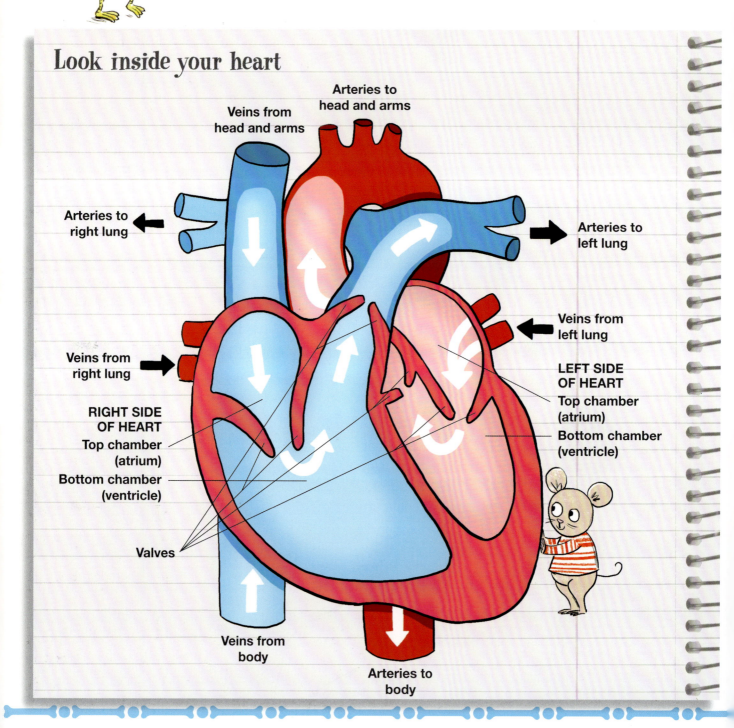

Veins from head and arms

Arteries to head and arms

Arteries to right lung

Arteries to left lung

Veins from right lung

Veins from left lung

RIGHT SIDE OF HEART
Top chamber (atrium)
Bottom chamber (ventricle)

LEFT SIDE OF HEART
Top chamber (atrium)
Bottom chamber (ventricle)

Valves

Veins from body

Arteries to body

Your heart is a very strong pump, which squeezes blood around your body. It has two sides and each side is divided into two chambers (spaces). The top chamber is called the atrium and the bottom chamber is called the ventricle. When blood has traveled around the body, and most of the oxygen has been used up, it flows into the right atrium and is squeezed on into the right ventricle. From there it shoots out toward your lungs. When it comes back from your lungs, it is full of oxygen.

It flows into the left atrium and then down into the left ventricle. From there it is given a really strong squeeze to send it traveling around the rest of your body. To make sure it only goes one way, there is a valve between the atrium and ventricle on each side of the heart.

Using the activities in the next few pages, first learn about what blood is and about how valves work in your heart and blood vessels; then go on to find out more about your heart and lungs.

Take a look at your blood

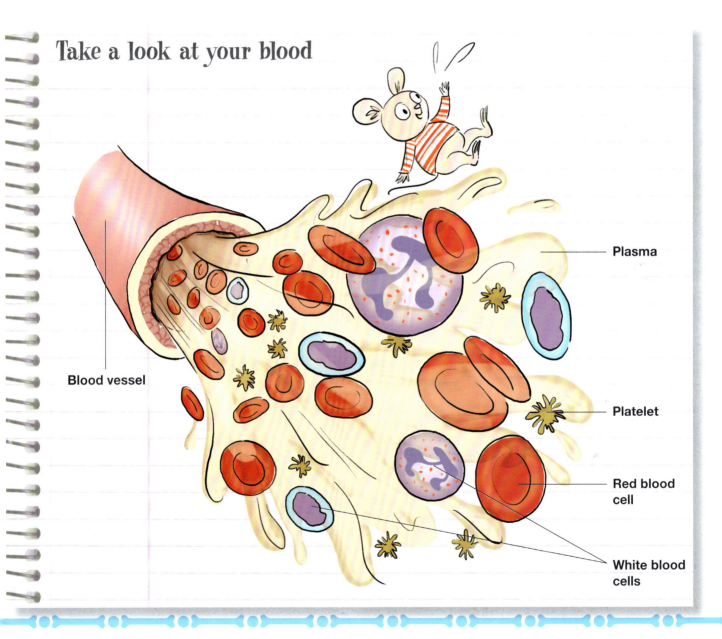

Blood vessel

Plasma

Platelet

Red blood cell

White blood cells

Make tasty fake blood

Depending on your age and size, you will have between 3½ and 7 pints (2 and 4 liters) of blood in your body—the bigger you grow, the more blood you need. If you cut yourself, you will bleed, but what exactly is blood? It looks like a thick red liquid, but it is made up of four different parts, each with different jobs to do, as you'll discover by doing this activity to make tasty, fruit salad blood!

You will need

⅓ cup (75 g) golden superfine (caster) sugar

⅓ cup (75 g) white superfine (caster) sugar

¾ cup (150 ml) water

saucepan

1½ cups (200 g) raspberries (big ones if possible)

straight-sided tumbler

1 x 14-oz. (400-g) can of lychees

1 pomegranate

rolling pin

1 First make some sugar syrup. Put the water and both types of sugar in a pan and ask an adult to help you heat it gently. Stir until the sugar has dissolved. Turn up the heat and bring it to the boil. Turn the heat back down and let it simmer for one minute. Remove from the heat and let it cool.

2 Imagine a disc of modeling clay, which you squeeze between your finger and thumb so there is a dip each side. That's what red blood cells look like, but we're going to use raspberries to represent red blood cells, even though they are not quite the right shape. Cut each raspberry in half and put them in the tumbler to make a thick layer. In your blood, red blood cells carry oxygen to all the other cells in the body. When they are full of oxygen, they are bright red. When the oxygen is used up, they are darker purple color.

3 Pour the cooled syrup, which should be straw-colored, over the raspberries until the glass contains about half raspberries and half syrup. The syrup represents blood plasma. Just over half (55 percent) of your blood is plasma and this is what makes blood runny.

Plasma is mostly water, but it has lots of other things dissolved in it. Plasma's job is to transport nutrients to every cell of the body. It also carries salt and chemical messengers called hormones and it takes away carbon dioxide and other waste from the cells (see page 88).

4 Open the can of lychees and add 2–3 lychees to the glass. These represent white blood cells.

White blood cells are bigger than red cells and there are not nearly so many of them. Their job is to fight infections that try to invade your body.

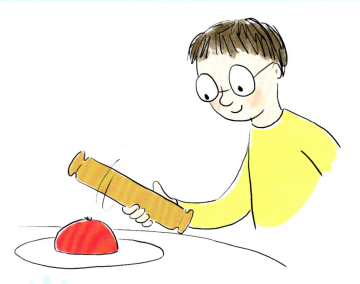

If someone cuts themself badly, call for help quickly. Cover the cut with something clean—a clean towel or tea towel if you haven't got a first-aid dressing—and keep pressing firmly on the cut to stop the bleeding. Bleeding stops more quickly if the heart has to pump the blood uphill, so make sure that the cut is held above the person's heart. If the cut is on their arm, get them to hold it up in the air; if it's on their leg, lie them down and raise their leg on a chair, with pillows, if necessary.

You know iron as a metal, but did you know that your body needs iron to make red blood cells. If you don't get enough, you will feel tired and won't have much energy. To get enough, you need to eat foods such as beans, nuts, red meat, eggs, dried fruits (raisins, apricots), and dark green leafy vegetables (cress, spinach, kale). Most breakfast cereals also have iron added to them—does yours?

5 Carefully cut the pomegranate in half (ask an adult to help if it's tough). Lay one half flat on a plate and hit it gently several times with a rolling pin. The seeds should fall out. Add some of the seeds to the mixture. These represent platelets and they are much smaller than red blood cells.

Platelets make blood clot (become solid) when you cut yourself— otherwise you would just keep bleeding.

6 Give everything a stir and then put it in the fridge for the flavors to mix before you eat it. If you wanted it to be more like blood, you would warm it up because blood, like the rest of your body, is always the same temperature—about 98.6°F (37°C), but your fruit salad will taste nicer cold!

Make a one-way valve

As we have seen in the diagram of the heart on page 82, valves are needed to stop blood flowing in the wrong direction. You can make a simple valve to see how they work.

You will need

scissors

thin latex glove or a balloon

drinking straw

sticky tape

cup of water

Your blood is always moving, traveling round and round your body in one big circuit, which is why it's called a circulatory system. Blood travels from the heart in big arteries. Imagine a car coming from a long way to reach your house. First it will travel on a freeway (motorway), then turn off onto a main road, then onto a smaller road, and then an even smaller one, until, eventually, the driver gets out of the car and walks up a path to your front door. A red blood cell does much the same. It starts off traveling along a main artery, but branches off into smaller and smaller arteries until it ends up in a tiny capillary.

Oxygen from the red blood cell then passes through the incredibly thin walls of the capillary into one of the cells of your body. Glucose, which is traveling in blood plasma, does the same. Once they have been off-loaded, the blood picks up waste products and carbon dioxide and begins its journey back to the heart, first along tiny venules then into bigger and bigger veins until it is on another freeway back to the heart. Blood in arteries is under huge pressure. If you cut one, the blood will spurt out. By the time it gets to veins, there is less push behind it so it needs a way to stop it going backward—it needs valves.

1 First, feel one side of your neck just below your jaw. You should be able to feel a pulse beating. This is the blood traveling along your carotid artery (a major freeway) to your brain. Now look at your wrist and see if you can see any veins. These look blue because there is less oxygen in the blood.

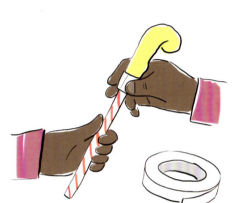

2 Cut the tip off a finger of the glove, then cut off the whole finger or cut the balloon in half.

3 Tape the open-ended finger over the end of the straw so that there is a big flap of floppy rubber over the end.

4 Put the balloon end of the straw into the cup of water and blow into the straw—it will be easy and you will make lots of bubbles. Now try sucking. Nothing comes back up the straw. Now just try blowing and sucking in the air—you'll find that you can blow but not suck. The rubber sucks back across the end of the straw and seals it. We have used air to show how the valve works, but the same kind of thing is happening in your veins all the time—blood flows easily one way, but valves drop across the veins to stop it flowing backward.

ROUND and ROUND it goes!

Find out about your heart

We have discovered what the heart looks like and how it pumps blood, but these simple activities will help you learn more about how it works. You will even be able to hear your own heartbeat, like a doctor does!

You will need

....

small funnel

piece of plastic tube
or hosepipe about
18 in. (46 cm) long

strong sticky tape

scissors

old tennis ball

Make a stethoscope

1 Push the plastic tube inside the tube of the funnel (or the funnel inside the tube if the tube is wider). Secure it tightly with sticky tape wrapped several times around it so there are no gaps.

2 Hold the funnel against your skin on the left side of your chest, where your heart is, and hold the end of the tube against your ear. Listen to your heartbeat. Move the funnel around until you can hear it clearly. The "lub-dub, lub-dub" heartbeat sound you can hear is the sound of the heart valves snapping shut. They don't shut at quite the same time, which is why you hear the double sound.

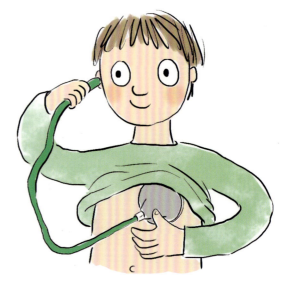

Lub-dub, lub-dub, LUB-DUB!

The more exercise you do, the more energy your body needs and so the faster the blood has to pump around your body bringing it oxygen and nutrients. Your heart muscle can never stop working, but you don't have to think about this. Your brain just makes sure it keeps pumping.

3 Use a timer and count how many times your heart beats in 15 seconds. Double this number and double again to find your heart rate for 1 minute. Now jump or dance around for 5 minutes then listen and count again. Work out your new heart rate. (Or you could use a heart rate app on a phone—there are lots of free ones available.) Every beat is a squeeze that shoots blood out and around your body or to your lungs.

find out about your heart 91

How does your heart work?

1 Now try something else. Carefully, use the point of a sharp pair of scissor to pierce a hole in the tennis ball (ask an adult to help you). Push the scissors right in and twist them around to make the hole a bit bigger.

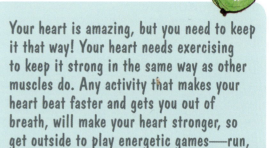

2 Fill your sink with water. Squeeze the ball to push out as much air as possible and then dunk it in the sink so that it fills up with water. Take it out of the water. Keeping it over the sink, squeeze the ball hard. The water will shoot out. Keep squeezing as you put it back in the water, then relax your squeeze and it will fill up again. This is how your heart works—it squeezes to push blood out and relaxes to let blood in. Empty the tennis ball.

3 Now hold it with your arm stretched out at shoulder height. Pretend your hand is a heart that has to keep squeezing the tennis ball every second (the tennis ball is a just a bit bigger than your heart, which is about the same size as your fist). How quickly do the muscles in your hand get tired? After 20 squeezes, 50 squeezes, 100 squeezes?

If your pulse rate is 80 beats a minute, your heart beats about 4,800 times in an hour, or 42,048,000 (that's more than 42 million) times in a year—and never gets tired. This shows how different and special your heart muscles are. Heart muscle is the third sort of muscle you have in your body (see page 52).

Make a model of your lungs

Take some really big breaths to fill your lungs with air. You can make a model of your lungs to find out how they work.

You will need

plastic bottle with a lid

sharp scissors

two balloons

strong sticky tape

hand drill (optional)

straw

some sticky tack

small elastic band

When you breathe in, imagine the air rushing in through your nose and down the tube (trachea) at the back of your throat. There the tube splits into two smaller tubes, one going to each lung. These tubes branch into even smaller tubes, so each lung looks a bit like an upside-down tree. The smallest branches end with tiny air sacs which are covered in tiny blood capillaries. Blood is pumped to the lung by the heart when it is full of carbon dioxide and almost empty of oxygen. The carbon dioxide moves out of the blood into the lung and you breathe it out. When you breathe in again, air fills the lungs and the oxygen from the air moves into the blood. The blood, now full of oxygen, travels to your heart to be pumped around your body.

 **1** Carefully cut the bottom off the plastic bottle—ask an adult to help you.

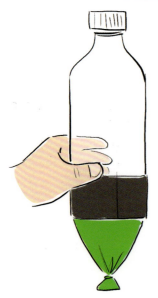

2 Tie a knot in the neck of one of the balloons. Cut open the bottom and then stretch the balloon across the open base of the bottle. It should be very tight. Secure it with strong sticky tape.

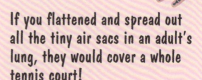

Fascinating Fact

If you flattened and spread out all the tiny air sacs in an adult's lung, they would cover a whole tennis court!

3 Make a hole in the bottle lid. You may need to ask an adult to help you with this—you can do it with pointy scissors, but using a hand drill is an easier way. The hole needs to be just big enough to push the straw through. Cut a piece of straw about 4 in. (10 cm) long and push it half through the lid. Mold some sticky tac around the hole to make an airtight seal.

4 Blow up the second balloon and then let the air out again (to make it easy to blow up again). Use an elastic band to attach the balloon to the straw below the lid. Twist the elastic over several times so that it is very tight. Push the balloon into the bottle and screw on the lid.

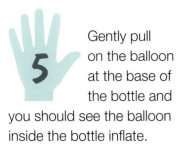

5 Gently pull on the balloon at the base of the bottle and you should see the balloon inside the bottle inflate.

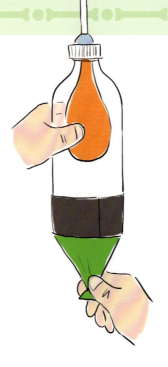

6 Pulling the balloon down makes a bigger space inside the bottle for the same amount of air, so the air pressure is lower. Air outside the bottle tries to get in to even out the pressure but it can only get into the balloon, so the balloon inflates. The same thing happens inside your chest.

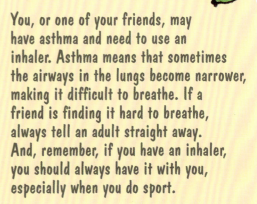

Health Tips

You, or one of your friends, may have asthma and need to use an inhaler. Asthma means that sometimes the airways in the lungs become narrower, making it difficult to breathe. If a friend is finding it hard to breathe, always tell an adult straight away. And, remember, if you have an inhaler, you should always have it with you, especially when you do sport.

Like with your heart, exercise that makes you out of breath is good for your lungs. To take care of your lungs, it is also important to avoid breathing in smoke—for example, from other people smoking in the same room as you, or being near a car exhaust.

Below your lungs you have a big muscle called the diaphragm, which is stretched across your chest. When it is relaxed, it is a dome shape, but when you breathe in, it flattens, pulling down just like the balloon. This makes a bigger space in your lungs. At the same time your ribs move up and out, making an even bigger space. Air rushes into your lungs to even out the pressure; in other words, you breathe in. Then the diaphragm relaxes and goes back to a dome shape, your ribs drop back, the pressure in the lungs increases, and the air rushes out—you breathe out.

Test your lungs

Your lungs will grow as you grow. The amount of air your lungs hold also increases when you are very fit, so there is no set amount for how much air your lungs will hold but it's fun to find out. This is easier to do with a friend.

1 Fill the bottle with water right to the very top and screw on the lid. Fill your sink with water until it is about 6 in. (14 cm) deep. Turn the bottle over and, with the top underwater, unscrew the lid. Get your friend to hold it upright.

You will need

2-quart (2-liter) drinks bottle with a lid

kitchen sink

length of plastic tubing

measuring pitcher (jug)

2 Keeping the bottle top under the water, push one end of the tube inside the bottle. Breathe in deeply and blow into the other end of the tube for as long as you can, until there is no air left in your lungs. All the air you breathe out will bubble to the top of the bottle.

3 Still keeping the top underwater, screw the cap back onto the bottle. Lift it out and turn it over. The amount of air in the bottle is the same as the amount of air you breathed out of your lungs. If you want to know the capacity of your lungs in fluid ounces (millilitres), pour the water that is left in the bottle into a measuring pitcher (jug) and measure how much there is. Subtract this amount from the amount that the bottle originally contained (2 quarts/liters) and you have your lung capacity. Now wash the tube and let your friend have a go.

YOUR EXCRETORY SYSTEM

Think about your home and the amount of waste that leaves it every week—from glass, plastic, cans, and paper for recycling, to vegetable peelings for the compost bin and other food waste and garbage. If it wasn't taken away it would soon fill up your house, go bad, and start to stink. Well, your body needs to get rid of waste, too!

Your body produces lots of waste when cells turn food to energy. We have seen how the lungs get rid of carbon dioxide, and the digestive system gets rid of poop. But there is more waste that your blood picks up and carries to your kidneys. The kidneys take out these waste products mixed with water and send them down a tube to your bladder —a bag with stretchy sides. When the bag is full, your brain tells you that you need to wee so you take yourself off to the bathroom (toilet). Urine is the proper name for wee and it comes out of your urethra. If your kidneys didn't work, waste would fill up your blood and poison you.

Health Tip

To keep your kidneys healthy, you need to drink plenty of water (but try to avoid too much soda/fizzy drink). If your wee starts to look quite dark or becomes a bit more smelly, this is a sign you need to drink more.

How your kidneys work

Kidneys are very complicated but you can get some idea of how they work from these neat experiments. Kidneys are filters. A filter is a layer of material with small holes in it. Tiny particles can move through the filter but bigger ones can't. Try out these filters.

1 Mix up some fine salt and some rice. How can you separate them again? Use a strainer (sieve) as a filter—the salt will drop through the holes and leave the rice in the sieve.

2 How about sand and salt? Mix together a few spoonfuls of each. How would you separate them? Answer: add a little warm water and stir. This will dissolve the salt, which means it breaks into much tinier particles which are invisible in the water. Line the strainer (sieve) with a piece of paper towel (a coffee filter is even better if you have one), put it over a shallow dish, and slowly pour the mixture onto it. The salt and water will pass through the microscopic holes in the paper and the sand will stay on top. If you leave the salty water somewhere warm, the water will evaporate and you'll get nice salt crystals.

3 Now for the filter, which is more like a kidney. Put on gloves and an apron for this and ask an adult to help you because the iodine will stain your fingers and clothes.

You will need

....

fine salt

small amount of dry rice

strainer (sieve)

shallow bowl

small amount of sand

paper towel (or a coffee filter)

rubber gloves

apron

large glass jar

cornstarch (cornflour)

teaspoon

tablespoon

iodine solution (available from some pharmacies or ask your doctor for a few drops in a glass bottle)

dropper

very small ziplock bag

In a large glass jar, mix 2 teaspoons of cornstarch (cornflour) with a tablespoon of water and stir until it is runny. Then add another cupful of water.

Using the dropper, put two squirts of iodine into the ziplock bag. Seal it and turn it upside down to check there are no leaks.

Drop it into the jar with the cornstarch and leave it for about half an hour.

With your gloves and apron on, pull the bag out of the jar. It will be covered in a layer of dark purple and the purple will be spreading out into the white cornstarch mixture. There is a chemical reaction between iodine and cornstarch, which makes it change color. But the iodine was in the bag! Nothing can get through plastic, can it? The change of color shows that unlike water, iodine can get through plastic just like the waste products in your blood can pass through the special tissue in your kidney to make urine.

If you want to prove that waste products really do get from your food through your blood to your kidneys and out in your wee, either eat some asparagus (just one or two pieces is enough) or some beets (beetroot)—a big serving of this. After eating asparagus, your wee will probably smell really weird—that's because of a waste product from asparagus that has got into your urine (a few people can't smell it). After eating beets, you may find you have pink wee as well as red poop. Beets contains a very strong dye that comes through both!

YOUR IMMUNE SYSTEM

Out in the world, there are loads of microscopically small living things—bacteria, viruses, and fungi (together called "pathogens"), which would make you ill if they got inside your body. The body has lots of ways to stop them, using its immune system.

Your first defence is your skin. You are completely wrapped up in skin and the pathogens can't get through it. However, there have to be openings in this wrapping so we can breathe, eat, hear, see, wee, and poop, and these opening are like doorways for pathogens to get in. So, wherever there are openings, there have to be other defences. Earwax and tiny hairs protect your ears, tears wash your eyes, saliva in your mouth contains anti-bacterial chemicals, and mucous (a slimy antibacterial liquid) protects other openings, especially your nose which, as you know, makes snot!

Look up your nose and you will see lots of hairs. These are there to trap dust, pollen, and the pathogens that make us ill. When snot runs down your nose, it picks up these nasties as it passes over the hairs and they end up on a tissue when you blow your nose, or, if you sneeze without a tissue, on other side of the room! If you have a cold, much more snot comes down your nose and it can be yellow or green. Some scientists have found that mucous from your nose can travel for about 15 ft. (4.5 m) from your nose when you sneeze so it may well end up on someone else, passing all your nasty bacteria onto them. That's why you should always sneeze into a tissue or into your arm.

Health Tips

Wash your hands really well every time you go to the toilet. Use soap and hot water and dry them afterward. That way you will wash off all the bacteria you have picked up from door handles, toilet flushes, faucets (taps), handrails, and other people's hands, and you are less likely to get ill.

A cut or a scab is a break in the protective barrier of your skin and could let in harmful pathogens. Clean any small cuts under a faucet (tap) and cover them with a plaster. Let an adult know if a cut becomes redder or has yellowish pus coming out—these are signs of infection.

Making snot!

To understand more about what snot is (and to gross out your friends), make some fake snot and then find out why you should never sneeze into your hand.

You will need

kettle

2 small bowls

3 packets of unflavored gelatine

fork

¼ cup (4 tablespoons) corn (golden) syrup

green food coloring

Vaseline

glitter

1 Ask an adult to help you heat water in a kettle until it is very hot, but not quite boiling. Pour half a cup of the almost boiling water into a bowl and sprinkle on the three packets of gelatine. Stir the powder in with a fork and then leave to soften for 5 minutes.

2 Put the corn (golden) syrup into another bowl.

3 Stir the gelatine mix with a fork until all the lumps have gone and then slowly add it to the corn syrup until your mixture looks like snot. Use a fork to stir it, as it will pull out long strands of snot. Add a few drops of green food coloring to make it even more disgusting. This looks like snot because it is made of the same ingredients as snot—protein, sugar, and water. They are different types of protein and sugar, but snot has a very similar chemical make-up.

4 Now wipe a very thin smear of Vaseline onto a door handle that everyone in your family uses a lot. Sprinkle a thin layer of glitter all over it—it should stick to the Vaseline. Don't tell anyone.

5 After a while get everyone to check their hands to see if there is glitter on them. Become a detective and check other places to find how far the glitter has spread. Imagine that you had a cold and had sneezed into your hand and then opened a door. The bacteria and viruses from your snot would have been wiped onto the door handle. The next person who opened the door would have got it on their hands and spread it further and probably caught your cold. This is why you should never sneeze into your hand—unless you are going to wash it straight away!

Model bacteria and viruses

In this activity you can have fun making models of some of the nastiest things in the world—the viruses and bacteria that cause disease. Then you can find out how many of these diseases you have been vaccinated against.

On every pathogen is a tiny part called an antigen, which cells in your body can recognize as a threat. If a pathogen gets inside your body, a powerful defence system called the immune system is activated. White blood cells (page 83) are part of this defence system. One type destroys invaders, while the other type allows the body to remember and recognize invaders that have got in before, so they can be fought off more easily. That's why if you have had chicken pox once, you are unlikely to get it again. The white blood cells recognize the virus and attack it before it has a chance to make you ill.

If you had lived 200 years ago, there is a good chance that you or your brother and sisters would have died of one of the many nasty diseases that were common then, diseases such as polio or diphtheria which you have probably never heard of. The reason why they have disappeared is vaccination. When you are vaccinated, you are given a shot (injection) of a little bit of the disease which has been made safe. It is a bit like putting up wanted posters all over your body. The body learns to recognize these nasty invaders and if it spots one inside your body, the whole of the body's defence system fights it off.

You will need

modeling clay in lots of different colors

pipe cleaners

nylon fishing line

scissors

Health Tip

Sometimes the body's defense system gets it wrong and begins fighting against harmless invaders. That's what an allergy is. For instance hay fever is an allergy to pollen from flowering plants. Hay fever is upsetting and annoying because you sneeze and your eyes itch. Other allergies are much more serious and can be very dangerous. If you have an Epipen because of an allergy, make sure you always carry it with you and make sure that people you are with know about it.

Fascinating Fact

Did you know that one disease has been wiped out completely from the whole world because of vaccination? Smallpox which was a bit like chicken pox but much worse—it killed or left a person horribly scarred—has now, thankfully, disappeared.

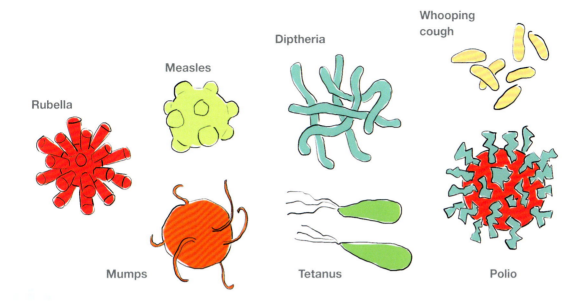

Rubella

Measles

Diptheria

Whooping cough

Mumps

Tetanus

Polio

1 Look at the pictures of viruses and bacteria. Scientists had to use very powerful electron microscopes to photograph them and then used computers to make them into pictures we can understand. Viruses and bacteria are too small to be colored, but color helps us recognize which is which.

2 Choose a virus or bacteria and begin to model it out of clay. Most start with a ball, some with a sausage.

3 Then add on all the extras. Snip off small pieces of pipe cleaners to make the stalks with blobs on the end. Use fishing line for the tails called flagella.

4 Ask your parents or carers which vaccinations you have had. Match them up with the models you have made. Find out whether you have had any other vaccines. Although it's sometimes not very nice having injections, it is very important to be vaccinated.

chapter 4

Your Control Center

In this chapter, you can discover a little about the most complicated thing in the universe—your incredible brain, with its billions of connections making all your memories, thoughts, and dreams, and keeping your whole body working.

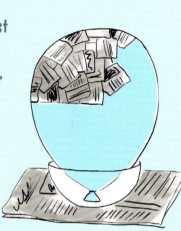

YOUR BRAIN 108

Make a brain hat 110

How fast are your reaction times? 114

YOUR NERVOUS SYSTEM 116

Make a pipe cleaner neuron 117

Billions of connections 119

Memory game 122

A dream diary 124

Confusing your brain 126

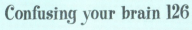

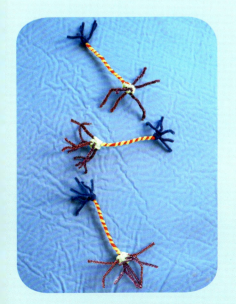

YOUR BRAIN

The human brain is amazing. It looks like soft, gray putty all folded up into hills and valleys, but it acts like a super, super, super computer, which is doing millions of incredibly complicated things all the time. Scientists are only just beginning to understand a little bit about how it works.

The brain is made up of many parts, all with different jobs to do, as you can see in the diagram opposite of a brain cut in half.

Cerebrum This is the biggest part. When you want to move, the cerebrum makes this happen. It also controls all your thoughts, your ability to work things out, your memories, your speech, your emotions, and it uses all your sense data to connect you with the world.

Brain stem This connects the rest of the brain to the spinal cord, which runs right down your neck and back inside your spinal column. The brain stem is in charge of keeping your body alive by controlling processes like breathing, digesting food, and making sure your heart is beating at the right speed.

Pituitary gland This releases chemical messengers called hormones. Among other things, these will make sure you keep growing and will start the changes that turn you from a child to an adult (puberty).

Hypothalamus This releases hormones that control your temperature and keeps it at about 98.6°F (37°C). If your body is too hot. the hypothalamus tells it to sweat; if it's too cold. it will give you goosebumps and start you shivering. It also controls your appetite, your sleep patterns, and when you get thirsty.

Cerebellum This controls balance, movement, and coordination (how your muscles work together).

Think about some of the things your brain does.
• You are your brain—everything you think and feel comes from your brain.
• Your brain controls the workings of your whole body—your heart, your lungs, your digestive system, and everything else depend on your brain to tell them what to do.
• Your brain has to interpret all the sense data that comes in from your eyes, ears, nose, tongue, and skin (see Chapter 1).
• Your brain controls every movement you decide to make.
• Your brain maps your world so you know where you are.

• Your brain understands time.
• Your brain lets you plan and calculate and work things out.
• Your brain contains all your memories.
• Your brain controls all your emotions.
• Your brain understands language; maybe just one or maybe several.
• Your brain coordinates all the skills you have ever learned, from speaking and walking, to reading, writing, playing the piano, or kicking a football.
• Your brain can imagine the future and make up stories.
• Your brain can create dreams.

Look inside your brain

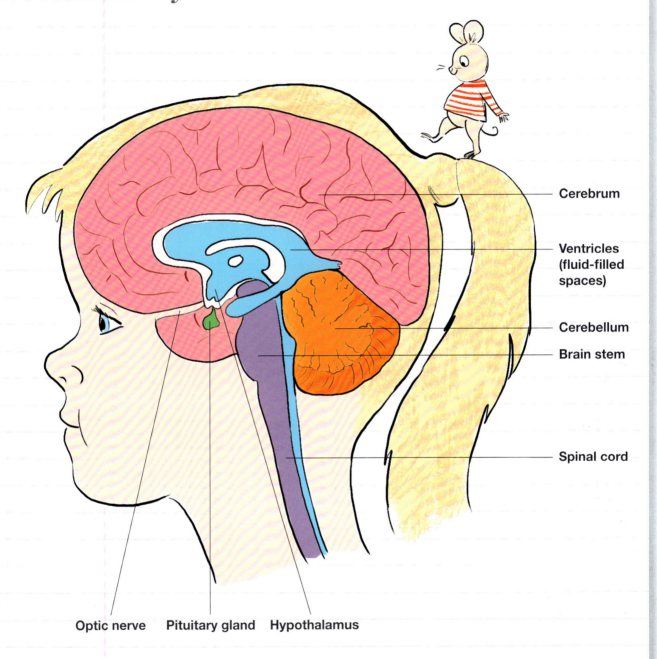

Cerebrum

Ventricles
(fluid-filled
spaces)

Cerebellum

Brain stem

Spinal cord

Optic nerve   Pituitary gland   Hypothalamus

Make a brain hat

Make a brain hat to show which area of the very top layer of your brain—your cerebral cortex—does what. Then, for instance, when you speak, you can point (using the power of several other areas of your brain) and say, "This part is working now!"

Some people say that one side of your brain can be more in control than the other. Those whose left side is more in control are supposed to be good at mathematics and science, and those whose right side is more in control are supposed to be good at creative subjects, such as art and music. But this is a myth! Don't let anyone tell you that your brain only allows you to be good at one of these areas. However, the left side does control and sense the right side of your body and the right side controls and senses the left side of your body.

Of course most of your brain is underneath the cerebral cortex and that keeps working all the time too. The brain hat is only a guide to what is going on, but it's cool to make and wear.

You will need

....

large round balloon

newspaper

white PVA glue

2 small bowls

white paper (recycle old computer printouts)

pencil

acrylic paints

paintbrushes

black markers

1 Prepare a messy area—spread out some sheets of newspaper to protect the work surface and put on an apron.

2 Blow up the balloon so it is as big as your head. Place it on top of a small bowl, tied end down, to hold it steady.

3 Pour some PVA glue into the other bowl and mix in about the same amount of water to thin it. Tear some newspaper into strips, and then tear the strips into rough pieces about 1½ in. (4 cm) square.

4 Dip a square into the glue and then stick it down on the balloon. Keep going, dipping and sticking, overlapping each square with the next. You only need cover the balloon down to its widest point to make a hat.

5 Stick two layers of newspaper pieces over the balloon. Now tear up the white paper and cover the newspaper layers with one layer of white paper. Smooth it down with your hands. Leave in a warm place to dry out completely.

6 Pop the balloon and remove it from inside the hat. Trim the edge with scissors to neaten it and try it for size.

7 Use a pencil to divide the hat into two halves down the middle—these will represent the left side and right side of your brain. Now mark out the areas on the brain as shown in the diagrams opposite. Paint the areas using the same four colors that we have used— not too dark as you need to write on them afterward.

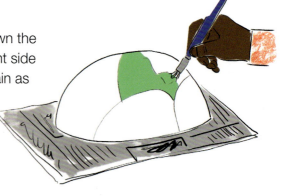

8 When the hat is dry, use marker pens to label each area on the right side of the brain hat with its correct name following this key: **pink** = frontal lobe, **green** = parietal lobe, **blue** = occipital lobe, **yellow** = temporal lobe. Remember that the pink frontal lobe is the front of the hat.

9 Now photocopy the symbols (right) and cut them out. Stick the symbols for what each area does on the left side of the brain, following the diagram for the left side of the brain.

Top diagram

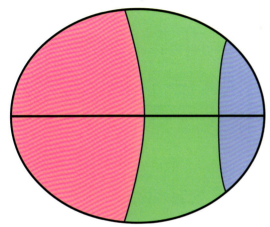

Right diagram

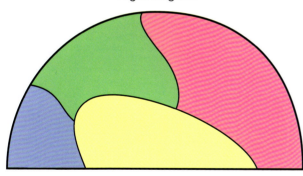

Left diagram

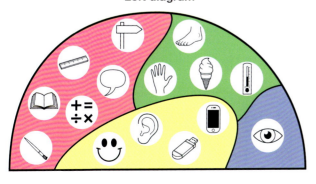

Key to symbols

Eye movement (understanding where you are)

Speech

Planning

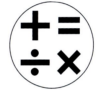

Reasoning and calculating

Concentrating

Creativity

Emotion

Hearing

Memory

Understanding language

Sight and understanding what you see

Movement

Taste

Temperature

Touch

How fast are your reaction times?

This activity tests how quickly your brain works. What you do is catch a ruler that someone else has dropped. Messages have to travel along nerves from your eyes to your brain and back to your hand. How long do they take? Try this reaction time test to find out.

You will need

....

friend
ruler

Fascinating Fact

If someone pretends to hit your face, you will blink. This is a reflex that protects your eyes. Another reflex makes your pupils contract in bright light (see page 13) or makes you pull your hand away when you touch something hot. It is a quicker movement than one you decide to do (a voluntary movement) because the signals don't go through your cerebrum (conscious brain), but just travel through your brain stem or your spinal cord instead.

Doctors may test one of your reflexes by tapping your knee with a hammer. Try it. Sit down and cross your legs. Tap the knee of your top leg with the edge of a ruler and watch your lower leg jerk up!

1 Hold the ruler between your finger and thumb at the opposite end to the zero (most rulers work both ways). Tell your friend that you will drop the ruler within the next ten seconds and they must try to catch it. Your friend should hold their hand at the bottom of the ruler so that it will drop between their finger and thumb.

2 Drop the ruler. Look at how far the ruler dropped before your friend caught it. Read the measurement in the middle of their thumb, reading up from zero at the bottom. The higher the measurement, the further the ruler dropped and the slower the reaction time. Try it a few times and see if their reaction time improves. Now swap around and try catching yourself.

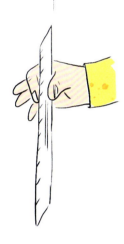

The light hits the back of your retina where light sensitive cells send electrical signals along the optic nerve to your brain (see page 109). The brain combines these signals with your thoughts about wanting to catch the ruler and then sends signals that travel down your spinal cord, along the nerves in your arm to the muscles in your hand, telling them to contract.

Fascinating Fact

An athlete's reaction time to a starting pistol can make the difference to how well they do in a race. Athletes are timed electronically, otherwise the reaction time of the person pressing the timer button would affect the results.

3 You can convert the measurement into time if you like. If you caught the ruler at 2 in. (5 cm), your reaction time was very fast at about 0.1 seconds. At 4 in. (10 cm) it was 0.14 seconds, 6 in. (15 cm) 0.17 seconds, 8 in. (20 cm) 0.2 seconds, 10 in. (25.5 cm) 0.23 seconds, 12 in. (30.5 cm) 0.25 seconds.

Who has the QUICKEST reaction times?

YOUR NERVOUS SYSTEM

The brain is the control center for the whole body, but it isn't a wireless system. Signals run to and from the brain along nerves that are made out of cells called neurons. The brain and spinal cord (which are also made out of neurons) are called the central nervous system; the nerves that connect them to the rest of the body are called the peripheral nervous system.

Look at neurons

In the peripheral nervous system, there are motor neurons that carry signals from the brain to the muscles telling them to expand or contract (see page 52), so you can move. There are also sensory neurons that carry signals back from your sense organs to the brain, so that you know what is happening around you. In addition, there is a system of neurons that automatically keeps your body working—you don't have to think to make your heart beat!

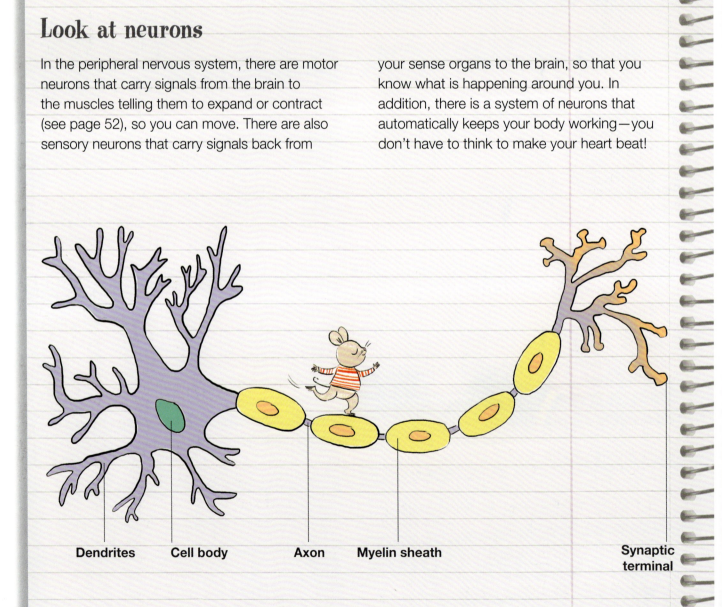

Dendrites   **Cell body**   **Axon**   **Myelin sheath**   **Synaptic terminal**

Make a pipe cleaner neuron

To understand how neurons work it helps to have a model. Make two neurons to understand properly—there are about a hundred billion of them in your body!

You will need

pipe cleaners in five different colors

scissors

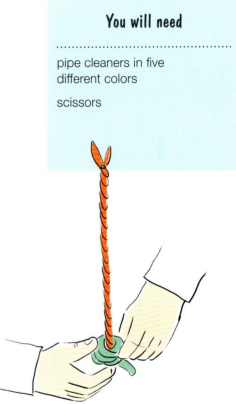

1 Take one pipe cleaner and fold it in half. This will be the cell body. Take a different colored pipe cleaner, fold this one in half, link it with the other one, and then twist the two ends together. This is the axon. Twist the cell body into a loose ball at the end of the axon (shown in green here).

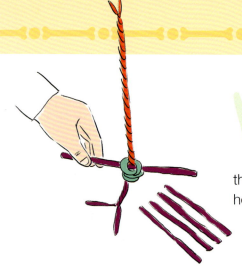

Take three pipe cleaners in a different color for the dendrites. Cut them in half. Push each of them through the cell body, fold in half, and twist together tightly for about half their length, leaving the ends separate. Twist them around into wild shapes. Then squash the cell body tight to hold them in place.

Choose a fourth color for the myelin sheath. Wrap it around the axon, but leave gaps so you can still see the axon.

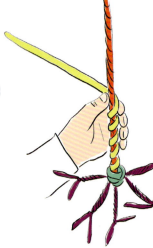

Fold the axon back a little way and wind it around itself to make a loop. Cut the fifth color pipe cleaner in half. Thread one half through the loop in the axon and twist it into a loose ball around the end of the axon like you did for the cell body. Thread through some shorter pieces of the same color, half twisting them together in the same way as you did for the dendrites. The ends of these are the synaptic terminals.

Make a second neuron. Put the two neurons end to end so that the synaptic terminal of one doesn't quite touch the dendrites of the other.

Electrical signals whizz along the axon to the synaptic terminal where chemical messengers are released. These jump across the tiny gap called a synapse between one neuron and the next. The chemical message is picked up by the wavy dendrites which change the chemical message back into an electrical signal to whizz along the next axon and so it continues from your brain to wherever the message needs to go. If you were doing the reaction time activity (see page 114), the signal would need to travel to your hand muscles. The myelin sheath around the axon makes the electrical signal travel faster.

Billions of connections

You have billions of neurons in your brain and nervous system and each neuron connects with other neurons. Every time you learn something or remember something, more connections are made between different neurons in your brain.

A hundred billion is the number of neurons that scientists estimate you have in your brain and you can multiply that number by millions more to find out the number of connections.

Even with just a few connections, things quickly get complicated as you can see with this activity. You can do it in two ways: you can either use a needle and colored yarn to join holes in the card or join the dots with colored pencils and a ruler. Imagine the dots are neurons. The colored yarns or lines are connections. Both look pretty impressive.

You will need

Either:
small piece of stiff card
ruler and pencil
2-hole punch
blunt needle with a big eye
lots of different colored yarns
sticky tape
scissors

Or:
paper
ruler
colored pencils or fine pens

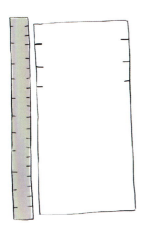

1 Cut a rectangle of card about 4 in. (10 cm) wide and 8 in. (20 cm) long. Use a ruler and make a mark every ¾ in. (2 cm) down each side. Join up the first four pairs of marks across the card.

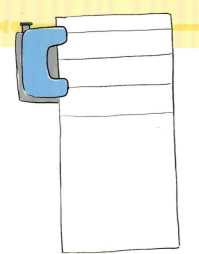

2 Push on the hole punch so the edge is against the first pencil line. Punch two holes. Move the hole punch along and line it up with the next pencil line and punch two more holes. Do this twice more and you will have eight evenly spaced holes. Now do the same on the opposite edge of the card so that there are another eight holes along this side. Turn the card over so the unmarked side is on top.

3 Thread the needle with a piece of colored yarn about 68 in. (170 cm) long. Tape the end to the back of your card. Bring the needle up through the first hole on the left side and then down through the first hole on the right side, then back up where you started and down second hole on the right side. Keep going until you have connections from the first hole on the left to all the holes on the right. Finish on the back, take off the needle, cut off the extra yarn, and secure the end with sticky tape. Each line of yarn represents a connection of one neuron with another.

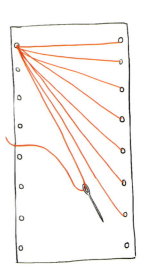

Fascinating Fact

It is easier for your brain to make neural connections when you are young than when you are older, so now is the time to learn difficult skills such as playing a musical instrument or learning a language. When you learn something new, neural pathways are set up in your brain and in time that activity becomes automatic—you can do it without thinking.

Fascinating Fact

Some neurons are several feet long! Other cells in your body are always being replaced but neurons must last you a lifetime. However, some get destroyed and you will end up with fewer neurons when you are old than you have now.

4 Choose the next color and repeat the process connecting the second hole on the left side with all the holes on the right side. Continue until all eight holes are connected with each other. You will have 64 connections and a cool piece of embroidery! Now try to imagine the connections if you had billions of holes down each side!

Variation

If you prefer to draw rather than sew, do almost the same. Measure and draw dots every ¾ in. (2 cm) all down each side and use a ruler and different colors to join each dot on the left side to all the dots on the right side. It soon gets complicated! Just imagine what is going on inside your brain!

Memory game

You can train your brain in lots of ways. Improving your memory is one of them and you can do this by playing a traditional game called Kim's game with your friends or family, in which you have to remember a tray full of objects.

To get good at Kim's game, you have to look at the objects really carefully (normally our brains only notice what they need to notice and ignore the rest). Saying the names out loud might help you remember, or you can quickly link the objects together in a crazy story. Train your brain to notice and remember like this and you could end up as a detective!

You will need

....

tray

about 20 small objects e.g. coin, pencil sharpener, toy car, key, scissors, pencil, button etc.

towel or other cloth

stopwatch or timer

paper and pencils

Fascinating Fact

Scientists discovered that you're more likely to remember something written down if it's in a hard-to-read font. It may be something worth trying next time you have a test, to find out if it works for you.

1 Spread all of the objects out on a tray.

2 Allow everyone to look at the objects for 1 minute, then cover up the tray with the towel.

Variation

One person, who isn't playing, removes an object or a few objects from the tray. Who is the first to name the missing object?

3 Now ask everyone to write down as many objects as they can remember. Who can remember the most?

How many things did you REMEMBER?

A dream diary

Why not keep a dream diary to find out how creative your brain really is? You may find that you begin to have lots more ideas for stories.

You will need

....

special notebook
pencil

Have you ever been asked to write a story at school and panicked because you had no idea what to write? This happens to all of us, but in fact your brain is brilliant at making up stories and does it every night in your dreams. Dreams are crazy. They mix up all the people and places you have ever known; they let you do impossible things like fly; they jump around from scene to scene and they are often difficult to remember when you wake up. Sometimes they are upsetting or scary (nightmares); sometimes you have the same dream over and over. Scientists still don't really know why we dream. Some think it is your brain's way of making sense of what has happened to you during the day and helping to store the important stuff.

1 Keep your notebook and pencil by your bed.

2 As soon as you wake up, write down any dream that you remember, however crazy. Don't do anything else before you write it down because that will push it out of your memory and don't worry about spelling or handwriting or punctuation. Only you should ever read it.

3 Try to draw one picture of something you can remember from your dream.

Health Tips

Everyone needs sleep but children need more than adults. You should be sleeping for 10–11 hours every night. If you don't get enough sleep, you will find it more difficult to think clearly and more difficult to learn; your reaction times will be slower, so you will be less good at sport and computer games; you will get into arguments more easily; you'll make mistakes and may be clumsier. You may also grow more slowly and be more likely to get ill. So it's worth getting to bed earlier. Late bedtimes aren't cool.

Some children find it hard to get to sleep and that can be upsetting. These tips can help:

• Go to bed and get up at the same time every day. Your brain learns when it's time to sleep.

• Keep your bedroom cool, quiet, and dark. Have just a small nightlight if you need one.

• Switch off the TV, computer, or video games 2 hours before bedtime. Light from computers messes up the chemical in your brain that makes you sleep.

• If you have a phone, leave it in the kitchen so you are not tempted to look at it.

• Don't rush around before bed. Do calm activities. Read, listen to stories, play quiet games.

• Don't eat a big meal close to bedtime or drink sodas. Milk, especially warm milk, can help you sleep.

Confusing your brain

One of the ways we can learn about how our brains work is by looking at pictures or words that confuse our brains. Try the ones below. There are lots more online—for example, search for "optical illusion elephant's legs" and "optical illusion dalmation dog."

Moving images

Is this pattern really moving on the page? Obviously not. Scientists are not completely sure how this works, but it may have something to do with being able to see bright colors a little quicker than dark colors, which makes patterns appear to move.

Optical illusion

Which is bigger? The black circle on the left or the black circle on the right?

The right dot looks bigger but it isn't, it's the same size. Your brain compares the dot with the size of the circle around it. In a small circle the dot looks bigger.

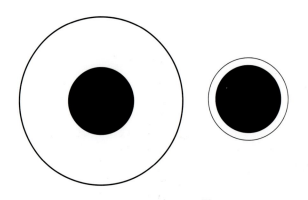

Index

A

air pressure 23
allergies 104
anus 67
appendix 67
arms
   bones 39
   muscles 52–53, 56
arteries 67, 68, 82, 88, 89
asthma 96
astronauts 40
atrium 82, 83
auditory canal 18
axon 116, 117, 118

B

bacteria 66, 77
   immune system 101, 104–5
   in intestines 75, 77
   on skin 30
   on teeth 72
balance 18, 21–22, 54, 55, 108
bicep 52–53, 56
bladder 67, 98
blind spot 16
blinking 12, 13, 114
blood 82–87
   cells 66, 83, 84, 86, 88, 104
   circulation 82–83, 88–89, 94
   made in bones 38
   nutrients 77, 86
   waste products 98–100
bones
   broken 44–47
   ear 19
   exercise 54
   function 38
   growing 54
   in hand 39, 59–60
   joints 43
   skeleton 38–39
   vitamins/minerals 42
brain 66, 107–9
   cerebral cortex hat 110–13
   confusing 126
   connections 119–21
   dreams 108, 124
   memory 108, 113, 122–23
   nervous system 116–21

reaction times 114–15, 118
   stem 108, 109, 114
breathing 80, 92, 94, 96, 97, 108

C

calcium 42, 68
canine teeth 70
carbon dioxide 72, 86, 88, 94
carpals 39, 59
cells 66, 116, 117, 118
cerebellum/cerebrum 108, 109
chyme 76
circulation 82–83, 88
clavicle 39
coccyx 39, 48
cochlea 18, 20
constipation 75
cooling down 35
cornea 10, 12
cuts 87, 101

D

dendrites 116, 118
dentin 68
dermis 28
diaphragm 67, 96
digestive system 66–79, 108
   gut string model 78–81
   poop 74–77
   teeth 68–71
disease 104, 105
dreams 108, 124–25
drinking water 75, 98

E

ear drum 18, 20, 21
ears 18–23, 101, 113
enamel 68
epidermis 28
epiglottis 24, 80
esophagus 24, 67, 76, 78
Eustachian tube 18, 23, 24
excretory system 98–100
exercise 35, 54–55, 91, 92, 108, 115
eyebrow 11, 34
eyelashes 12
eyelids 12, 30

eyes 10–17
   and balance 22
   brain role 113, 114, 115, 126
   color 13
   eye socket 39
   testing 16–17

F

face 11, 53, 58
feet 30, 39
femur 39
fiber 75
fibula 39
fingers 30, 39, 59
first aid 80, 87, 101
fitness 54–55
flexibility 50–51, 55
food
   containing iron 87
   digestive system 66, 75
   taste and smell 24–27, 113
fungi 101

G

gallbladder 67
goosebumps 33, 108

H

hair 28, 33–34, 101
hands 59–63
   bones 39, 59
   nerves 30
   robot hand 60–63
   washing 101
hearing 18–20, 21, 113
heart 66, 67, 82–83
   how it works 90–93, 108
   valves 82, 83, 88–89, 90
hormones 86, 108
humerus 39
hypothalamus 108, 109

I

immune system 66, 101–5
incisors 70
incus 18
infections 86, 101, 103, 104
inner ear 18

intestines 67, 76–77, 80–81
iris 10, 12
iron 87

J

jaw muscle 58
joints 43, 54

K

kidneys 66, 67, 98, 99–100
Kim's game 122–23

L

larynx 20, 24
legs 30, 39, 58, 114
lens 10
ligaments 43
liver 66, 67, 77
lungs 66, 67, 83, 89, 94–97, 108

M

malleus 18
memory 108, 113, 122–23
metacarpals 39, 59
metatarsals 39
middle ear 18, 20, 23
molars 70, 75
mucous 101, 102
muscles 38, 52–58
   arm 52–53, 56
   brain role 108, 116
   exercising 54–55
   hand 60, 63
   heart 92
   model 56–58
   skeletal 52
   smooth 77
myelin sheath 116, 118

Credits

N

nasal cavity 24
neck vertebrae 39
nerves
    optic 10, 16, 109, 115
    in skin 28, 29, 30, 31, 32
    spinal cord 48, 114, 115, 116
    in teeth 68
nervous system 116–26
neurons 66, 116–21
nose
    smell 24, 25–26, 27
    snot 101, 102–3

O

oesophagus 24, 67, 76, 78
optical illusion 126
optic nerve 10, 16, 109, 115
oral cavity 24
organs 38, 66–67
outer ear 18
oxygen 83, 88, 89, 94

P

pancreas 67, 77
patella 39
pathogens 101, 104
pelvis 38, 39
phalanges 39, 59
pinhole camera 14–15
pinna 18, 24
pituitary gland 108, 109
plaque 72–73
plasma 83, 86, 88
platelet 83, 87
poop 74–77
pre-molars 70
projects, difficulty 7
pulp 68
pupil 10, 12, 13, 114

R

radius 39, 59
reaction times 118
rectum 67
reflexes 114

retina 10, 16, 115
rib cage 38, 39, 96
road, crossing 17

S

saliva 75, 101
scapula 39
sebaceous gland 28
semicircular canals 18, 21, 22
senses
    brain role 108, 113, 116
    ears 18–23
    eyes 10–17
    smell 24, 25–26
    taste 26–27, 113
    touch 29–32, 113
sign language 59
singing 20
skeleton 38–49
skin 28–32
    body hair 28, 33–34
    cooling down 35
    immune system 101
    sunburn 35
    washing 35, 101
skull 38, 39, 110
sleep 127
sling, making 46–47
smell 24, 25–26, 27
snot 101, 102–3
sound 18–20, 21, 113
speech 20, 108, 110
spinal cord 48, 108, 109, 114, 115, 116
spine 38, 39, 48–51
spleen 67
sport 54–55, 92, 96, 108, 115
stapes 18
sternum 39
stethoscope 90–91
stomach 67, 76, 78
strength 54, 55, 92
subcutaneous tissue 28
sugar 26
sunburn 35
sunglasses 13
sweating 28, 35, 108
synaptic terminal 116, 118

T

tarsals 39
taste 26, 27, 113
tears 12, 101
teeth 24, 39, 68–71
    jaw muscle 58
    plaque 72–73
    and sugar 26
    vitamins/minerals 42
temperature
    of body 87, 108
    skin 31–32, 33
tendons 52, 63
thumb 63
tibia 39
tongue 24, 26
touch 29–32, 113
trachea 67, 80
triceps 52–53, 56

U

ulna 39, 59
ureter 67
urethra 67, 98
urine 98

V

vaccinations 104, 105
valve, heart 82, 83, 88–89, 90
veins 67, 82, 88, 89
ventricle 82, 83, 109
vertebrae 39, 48
viruses 101, 104–5
Vitamin D 35, 42
voice box 20, 24

W

washing 35, 101
wee 98
windpipe (trachea) 67, 80

All photography by **Terry Benson** unless specified below.

Drummond, Dylan pp.9, 30, 66

Getty Images/
Camille Tokerud Photography Inc. p.51
DRB5657 p.126
Klaus Vedfelt p.125
Lisa Pines p.44
Mike Kemp p.101
Nick David p.120
Thomas Barwick p.43
Thomas Northcut p.22

Heinze, Winifried p.98
Wreford, Polly p.123